INCREDIBLE
EDIBLES

43 FUN THINGS TO
GROW IN THE CITY

INCREDIBLE EDIBLES

43 FUN THINGS TO GROW IN THE CITY

SONIA DAY

PHOTOGRAPHY BARRIE MURDOCK

FIREFLY BOOKS

A FIREFLY BOOK

Published by Firefly Books Ltd. 2010

The publisher gratefully acknowledges the financial support for our publishing program by the Government of Canada through the Canada Book Fund as administered by the Department of Canadian Heritage.

First printing

Library and Archives Canada Cataloguing in Publication

Day, Sonia
Incredible edibles : 43 fun things to grow in the city /
Sonia Day ; photography Barrie Murdock.
Includes index.
ISBN-13: 978-1-55407-624-6
ISBN-10: 1-55407-624-2
1. Urban gardening. 2. Vegetable gardening.
3. Herb gardening. I. Murdock, Barrie, 1947- II. Title.
SB453.D375 2010   635.091732   C2009-907228-9

Publisher Cataloging-in-Publication Data (U.S.)

Day, Sonia.
Incredible edibles : 43 fun things to grow in the city /
Sonia Day ; photography Barrie Murdock.
[   ] p. : col. photos. ;   cm.
Includes index.
Summary: Instructions and gardening advice for cultivating vegetables, herbs and fruit, in back and front yards, on rooftops, balconies and other suitable spaces in the city. Includes profiles of specially selected easy-to-grow plants, with recipes and recommended plant and seed sources.
ISBN-13: 978-1-554076-246
ISBN-10: 1-55407-624-2
1. Vegetable gardening. 2. Urban gardening.
3. Organic gardening. I. Murdock, Barrie. II. Title.
635.0484 dc22   SB324.3D39   2010

Published in Canada by
Firefly Books Ltd.
66 Leek Crescent
Richmond Hill, Ontario L4B 1H1

Published in the United States by
Firefly Books (U.S.) Inc.
P.O. Box 1338, Ellicott Station
Buffalo, New York 14205

Cover design, interior design and production: Chris McCorkindale and Sue Breen
McCorkindale Advertising & Design
All photography by Barrie Murdock unless noted at page 124.

Printed in China

Note from the author

Gardeners are the most generous people on earth.
They always love sharing — not just their produce, but new ideas,
growing tips and recipes too. A big thank you to all those who have
contributed in many valuable ways to the preparation of this book.

Contents

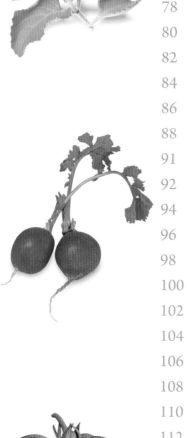

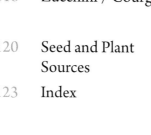

Introduction

Home-grown food. How enticing it sounds in this day and age. Luscious ripe tomatoes, instead of the cardboard kinds sold at the supermarket. Delectable salad greens that haven't been drenched in pesticides. Perfect little new potatoes, just dug up from crumbly brown soil. Fragrant leaves of basil and rosemary to snip into soups and pasta dishes....

In our increasingly overcrowded and polluted world, where plastic and concrete predominate, who hasn't dreamed of such things?

Bombarded as we are with bad news about climate change, environmental disasters and economic downturns — not to mention all those guilt trips about plastic-wrapped zucchini shipped thousands of miles from Guatemala — it's no surprise that people everywhere who have never planted a thing in their lives are now saying: "I want to grow my own food, because then what I'm putting into my body will be fresher, purer, better for the environment and safer."

This phenomenon has become so hot that sales of vegetable seeds are soaring. They've outstripped those of flowers for the first time since the back-to-the-land movement of the 1960s. Now, even Michele Obama is growing vegetables at the White House, looking for healthful locally grown food for her family, and Prince Charles has been into sustainable organic farming for a couple of decades, although on a bigger scale. Yet how feasible is our new-found fantasy? Doesn't cultivating food require tons of space and backbreaking hours of digging and weeding? Is "home-grown" a goal that the modern city dweller can realistically strive for?

The answer is: perhaps. And the keyword, if you want to do it, is "smaller." Smaller quantities, smaller kinds of veggies, smaller ways of growing them. Because in the past few years, gardening — and particularly vegetable gardening — has been quietly undergoing enormous changes to

Vegtable growing has changed since our grandparents' day. You can now find many more started plants in pots.

meet the demands of the way we live now. It's time to forget those old backyard veggie plots, the kind our grandparents toiled over, with onions, bush beans and beets planted in orderly rows — and a bottle of weed killer close at hand. They're as out of date as yesterday's French baguette. Today's urban gardeners, limited to smaller spaces than previous generations yet much more environmentally conscious, are discovering new, imaginative approaches to growing food.

Hand in hand with our changing attitudes have come dramatic differences to the selection of veggies, fruit and herbs available to home gardeners. Growers have — hallelujah — at last woken up to the fact that space is at a premium nowadays. As a consequence, they're coming out with more and more choices designed specifically for containers or small gardens. Just take a look at the seed catalogues. It's amazing how they've changed. You can now find at least a dozen container-friendly tomato varieties, midget melons and cucumbers that develop into bushes rather than vines. There are neat little heads of Tom Thumb lettuce capable of fitting into the palm of your hand, a delightfully diminutive eggplant whose long purple fruits grow not much bigger than a man's thumb, and summer (and winter) squashes that don't go berserk, sprawling everywhere and drowning us in those fabled zucchini torpedoes. Even better, the list of choices keeps getting longer and more varied every year.

However, that doesn't mean growing our own food has become a cakewalk. It wasn't years ago, and still isn't. All plants, edible or not, require TLC and they have their own particular likes and dislikes. Also, some vegetables — mostly the larger kinds — simply aren't suited to small urban spaces.

Period. So it's important to pick the right ones.

The good news is, though, that many delicious foodstuffs which we're accustomed to eating and using in cooking (plus other more novel ones) can be cultivated successfully in the city. In this book, I'll show you how — and which kinds to try. I've picked 43 edibles that adapt well to growing in containers and small gardens in average northern climates. Whether you live in a house with a regular garden, an apartment with a deck out back, a condo with a balcony, or you're part of a community gardening effort, any of these selections can be attempted by beginners with a minimum of hassle and expense.

I've made the instructions quick to read and down to earth. And none of our photos have been tinkered with using Photoshop — they show veggies, herbs and fruits as they really look, flaws and all. Included, too, are easy recipes and lots of tips, because I have personally tested (and eaten) everything I recommend in these pages.

For satisfaction, there's nothing like preparing a meal with herbs and veggies harvested from your own garden.

Now is a very good time to rethink our attitudes to food, where it comes from, and how we can play a part by growing some ourselves. Time and effort are necessary, of course, but taking the plunge into "incredible edibles" is a relaxing way to escape from the stresses of urban living. It's also fun, endlessly satisfying and, wow, how that home-grown produce will impress your friends.

And I guarantee one thing: pop a juicy cherry tomato — still warm from the sun and picked off the vine — into your mouth, and you won't ever want to settle for the supermarket kind again.

About the recipes in this book

I love to prepare and eat my own Incredible Edibles in a variety of ways, drawing from cuisines around the world. But I'm not a precise kind of cook. Nor are any of my friends. So my measurements aren't always exact. If your own measuring cups and spoons vary a bit from mine, it won't matter much. Bon appétit.

The Ten Commandments of Growing Food in the City

1 LET THERE BE LIGHT — PREFERABLY LOTS

The inescapable and annoying truth about veggies, herbs and fruit is that most need sun to grow well. At least six hours a day is best, although there are a few undemanding ones that will make do with less. (I've included them in this book.)

The "sun or forget it" rule is certainly a deterrent, because most of us aren't blessed with access to that kind of intense, uninterrupted light. In both cities and suburbs, there's almost always something casting shade at least part of the day. It could be the condo building next door, or overhanging trees, or the neighbor's privacy fence. Even her minivan, always parked in the same spot in the driveway, can present problems if it consistently stops the sun reaching the spot where you put in a couple of tomato plants.

What to do? Be inventive. Look around you. There may be a small sunny space that you haven't considered where it's possible to plant at least something — perhaps a few stalks of garlic or some runner beans. And think about growing up, not "out." (You can find so many climbing varieties of vegetables now.)

Don't write off the whole idea of growing your own food simply because you don't have room out back to create the kind of classic vegetable plot that our grandparents had. Hardly anyone does — and the whole idea is so yesterday anyway. There are other possibilities, if you seek them out.

Tomatoes are one of the easiest (and most popular) things to grow but they require plenty of sun to do well.

Around houses

- **Upstairs decks and balconies.** Great for growing food in containers because they're usually high off the ground and not shaded by trees or buildings.
- **Back fences, walls of garages and side walls of houses.** Often get far more sunshine than the interiors of backyards.
- **Front yards.** In bygone days, Italian and Portuguese immigrants (who've always been savvy about growing their own food) surprised their neighbors when they skipped having lawns out front of their modest city houses and planted grape vines and tomato plants instead. What smart folks. They realized early on that the front of a house is almost always sunnier than the back.

Even the tiniest place, like this balcony in Rome, can be used for growing food. (Left) Raised beds are a good choice in any location where it's difficult to improve the existing soil.

Around condos and apartment buildings

- **Balconies and terraces.** Those that face east, west and south are usually the best bets for growing food, but not always. If you're high in the sky and look smack south, it can get too hot, dry and windy up there for many things to survive. The same goes for rooftop gardens, where some kind of windbreak, along with a relentless watering regime, is usually necessary.
- **North-facing isn't necessarily out.** That's the real surprise. Balconies with a northerly aspect can prove to be good growing environments for veggies that don't mind some shade (like lettuce), because there's still a lot of light up there — usually bouncing off surrounding buildings — and the plants are shielded from the sun's relentless rays. They don't dry out too quickly and fare better than those forced to bake in southerly heat all day.

One condo dweller I know grows perfect lettuce every year in containers on his seventh-floor, north-facing balcony.

Around the city

Community gardens are a hot trend. So are urban agriculture activists, who keep pushing city poohbahs to open up more spaces. Check the possibilities. Get on waiting lists for an allotment or plot. Demand unfortunately outstrips supply almost everywhere, but that is changing as more and more city residents get the urge to grow and eat local.

Plots devoted to growing food are usually located in parks and urban wastelands, where enthusiasts frequently take it into their own hands to get things going — clearing out weedy, garbage-filled spaces that have been left vacant for years. Joining in is a great way to make new friends, enjoy exercise in the open air, and experience a sense of purpose and accomplishment — not to mention all that fresh, tasty food!

What to do first

Observe carefully the course of the sun over your home for a few days, whether you live in a house, apartment or condo. Make notes of the spots that get the most sunshine, how long the sun lingers there, and when it moves on.

Bear in mind that the sun shifts its position throughout the summer. In the northern hemisphere, by the end of June, it's going to rise and set much further north than it does right after the winter. Watch for obstructions that reduce the amount of light — usually tall buildings. Remember, too, that a big tree that's bare in April may cast dense shade by the time the growing season gets into full swing.

Cheat Mother Nature

You don't get enough sunlight for veggies anywhere? Don't despair. Artificial aids might help. Mirrors placed in strategic spots in gardens can direct a lot of sun to areas where it's lacking. So can panels of gatorboard or plywood covered in inexpensive kitchen foil.

Also: consider using containers placed on wheels. (There are many of these devices on the market now.) Move them around throughout the day to catch every ray of that precious sunshine.

Brick pathways between raised beds are a chore to install, but can be a good way to stop weeds becoming a nuisance.

2 SUPPLY GOOD SOIL

Before doing anything else, make sure that you provide plants with a good growing environment.

The old saying "tend the soil, not the plants" is particularly applicable to cultivating food. Almost all vegetables and fruits are greedy feeders. Their roots require a differing range of nutrients, whether they're planted in garden soil or a container filled with bagged mix. Without the right nutrients, your produce may be wizened, poorly formed or nonexistent, and it's more prone to attack by bugs and diseases. (Herbs, however, tend to be the exception. Some actually prefer poor soil, particularly if it's sandy. That's what makes them ideal starter plants for beginner gardeners.)

What to do
In an urban back or front garden

It's highly unlikely that the soil surrounding your home is the "perfect loam" that all experienced gardeners strive for. This is true whether you live in an old downtown house, where the nutrients on your lot were undoubtedly depleted long ago, or in a new subdivision, where developers have a nasty habit of stripping off every inch of topsoil, then restoring a skimpy layer after construction is over.

Whatever the location, it's a good idea to build up the soil before starting to grow anything. Do this by adding lots of compost to the areas intended for edibles — if you have any, that is. Since most of us don't (I've yet to meet a single gardener who ever makes enough compost for his/her garden), buy bagged composted manure at the garden center and work that in thoroughly. Sheep manure is the best to use. Horse manure tends to be too salty. Cattle manure packs fewer nutrients. Chicken manure falls somewhere in between. You may need to invest in a lot of bags, but it's worth it.

A load of manure from a friendly farmer — if you know one — is much cheaper than the bagged stuff and works wonders with many veggies. However, do not work raw, uncomposted manure into your garden in spring because it will burn plants and probably kill them. The time to spread raw manure on a veggie area is in the fall. Then leave it to "marinate" until spring. Bear in mind, though, that fresh manure stinks to high heaven. The no-longer-odiferous kind of composted manure from the garden center may keep you on friendlier terms with the neighbors.

If your soil seems impossibly poor, constructing a raised bed and filling it with bags of compost and potting soil may be the simplest option.

What to do
On a deck, balcony or rooftop
Getting the soil mix right for veggies, herbs and fruit planted in containers can actually be easier than in a conventional garden — because you work from scratch.

However, there's a bewildering variety of growing mixes offered in those big, shiny bags at garden centers nowadays — and many are vague and unhelpful as to exactly what they contain.

Plenty of worms are a sign that your soil is in good shape.

Read the labels. You'll find the main ingredient in most is peat moss. And because peat doesn't contain a lot of nutrients, mix makers supplement it with additives such as chemical slow-release fertilizers, organic fertilizers (a popular choice is seaweed), composted softwood bark, vermiculite

Check out coir
If soil is clayey and difficult to work with (that is, it clumps together in big hard chunks), adding another soil loosener besides compost is worthwhile. And if it's sandy, you probably need an additive too, to stop water draining away too fast.

What to use? Traditionally, peat moss was

ideal for both purposes. However, in our environmentally sensitive times, this has become a no-no. Although garden centers still sell great bales of peat moss every

spring, the fact is, by stripping bogs of peat we are eroding the world's wetlands — and they are as vital to our survival as rain forests.

So choose the "no guilt" option instead: coir. It's made from the ground-up fiber of coconuts. There are huge stockpiles of the stuff going begging in countries like Vietnam and India.

I find coir works better than peat moss at retaining water. Try it in containers. Although it can be argued that recycling coconut waste for gardens in the West isn't exactly environmentally friendly either, since it has to be shipped vast distances, this is surely preferable to wiping out irreplaceable peat bogs. Packaging coir creates jobs in impoverished parts of the world too.

Coir products can be hard to find at garden centers. Ask the manager to check this terrific additive out. If more people do, they'll become more readily available.

In most gardens, it's usually necessary to amend the soil with something to boost its nutrient content.

(which looks like nubbly bits of Styrofoam) or perlite (also nubbly, but a grayish color and made from heated lava rock), composted manure (usually from cattle or chickens) and bentonite clay, to retain water.

Some of these mixes do a good job. Most are pricey. Experiment. The costly ones aren't necessarily the best. And be wary of "all-purpose mixes" designed for vegetables, because they may work with some crops, but be disastrous with others. The ones that contain slow-release, nitrogen-heavy fertilizer give a boost to leafy crops such as spinach and lettuce, but may result in too many leaves on tomato plants and a shortage of fruit.

You'll also see a lot of bags labeled simply "potting soil." These can produce excellent or poor results, depending upon the company that packaged it. Again, experiment. Generally speaking, the pricier the potting soil, the better it will perform.

Whatever you buy, look for the words "sterile" or "weed free" on the bags. These products have been heated to 180°F / 82°C to kill bacteria, insect eggs and weed seeds that often lurk unseen in growing mixes and can wreak havoc in gardens.

Don't buy bags labeled "topsoil." These are generally cheaper, but topsoil is too heavy to use in containers.

Make your own mix

If you have lots of containers to fill, try it. The overall cost may be less. Find a big plastic container (an old kids' wading pool is ideal) and wear rubber gloves if you don't like getting your hands dirty. The trick is to combine the ingredients thoroughly, as if you're baking a cake.

Here are two recipes from avid container gardeners:

- Buy equal parts of potting soil, compressed or bagged coir, triple mix (which contains peat moss, soil and manure) and vermiculite. Keep mixing till everything looks "nice and crumbly."
- Combine equal parts of sheep manure, compressed or bagged coir, and a soil-less mix that contains vermiculite. Add a few handfuls of bonemeal.

Top up every spring

When vegetables are grown year after year in the same container, such as a built-in planter on a deck, it's imperative to change some of the soil every spring, because all the good stuff — those nutrients — will have been used up the previous year.

The easiest way is to scrape about 6 in. / 15 cm off the surface of the planter. Then add a layer of compost or potting soil. Work this in with a trowel and let it settle before planting anything new. If your yields were poor the previous season, refilling the entire container with fresh growing mix combined with compost may be necessary.

And do what farmers do: rotate your crops. For best results, try to avoid growing the same things in the same container year after year. Mix things up. This rule applies in regular gardens too.

3 CHOOSE THE RIGHT SPOT — OR POT

In a small urban garden, it's essential to pick the sunniest spot you can find. (See Commandment 1.)

However, when you're intending to cultivate food in a confined space, as in a container, something else besides the sun becomes equally important.

Your containers must be big enough. Most flowerpots, urns, planters, hanging baskets and window boxes available at garden centers look decorative, for sure. But they're often far too small — not wide, deep or long enough, or with thick sides and hardly any space left inside the container.

Vegetables and fruit must have room to spread their roots. (Salad greens and some drought-tolerant herbs are less fussy, surviving nicely in small, shallow containers.)

And all containers, irrespective of their size or shape, should have at least one drainage hole in the bottom. It's annoying how many lovely containers don't.

Some herbs will flourish in small pots, but most vegtables prefer lots of room. Give them the largest containers you can find.

Container choices — the good, the bad and the ugly

- **Terracotta containers**: Aesthetically pleasing, age well and are porous so plants can breathe. Some gardeners won't use anything else for herbs. Drawbacks: they're heavy, break easily and it's hard to find any container made of terracotta that's big enough for most vegetables.
- **Plastic flowerpots**: Cheap, effective, often the best bet. Choose white or terra-cotta colored pots over black ones, which tend to soak up too much heat from the sun. Again, they must be big, at least 12 in. / 30 cm across, for most veggies.
- **Discarded recycling bins**: Perfect, particularly for potatoes (see page 88) because they have deep, roomy interiors and are made of sturdy materials. If boxes have no drainage holes, punch some in the bottom with a sharp nail and hammer.
- **Window boxes**: Good for shallow-rooted salad greens but usually not deep enough for larger plants like tomatoes.
- **Whiskey barrels**: Fine for some veggies (one zucchini plant resplendent in a barrel looks great) but they're awkward to move around and have become pricey at garden centers.
- **Homemade wooden planter boxes**: Worth the effort if you're seriously into growing food. Make them wide, deep and from untreated wood. (Treated stuff will leach questionable chemicals into your carrots and onions.) Lining with Styrofoam sheeting is a good idea in cold areas. Non-toxic wood unfortunately splits and rots after a few years when used as a container for plants, because the interior is usually constantly damp. Make your boxes last longer by raising them a bit off the ground on blocks of wood, so air can pass underneath and they dry out quicker.
- **Grow bags**: Okay for tomato plants. Good in a temporary situation. But they tend to sprawl and split open and make a mess.
- **Hanging baskets**: Pass on these, unless you're willing to haul out hoses and watering cans nonstop. Veggies need lots of water. Baskets tend to dry out in a flash.

4 PICK THINGS THAT GROW WELL IN THE CITY

It's easy to get carried away when looking at seed catalogues. We thumb through them in winter when the weather is usually ghastly outside — and how seductive all those pretty pictures look. Luscious red tomatoes, big as tennis balls, bright green beans, perfect heads of cauliflower, elegant cucumbers, yellow and orange winter squash in all shapes and sizes....

Yet caution, folks. Although seductive, many of these offerings are difficult — or plain impossible — to grow in small spaces. For success, it's crucial

Understanding maturity dates

All good seed catalogues tell you how long it takes veggies to reach maturity — that is, produce ripe crops, ready to harvest. This is usually listed somewhere in the blurb. For instance: Celeriac Brilliant (110 days). While this information is useful, don't regard it as gospel. Weather plays a huge role in determining the actual date when any plant reaches its mature size. Out-of-the-ordinary conditions can skew the timing considerably.

During hot springs and summers, everything ripens much quicker. Some crops also get a growth boost from heavy rain. However, if there's a prolonged cool, gray spell, maturity for sun-loving veggies can be delayed for weeks. You'll be biting your nails, wondering if those darn tomatoes are going to turn red before fall frosts arrive.

Because actual maturity is unpredictable, unless you can start the seeds indoors during the winter, avoid growing anything in a northern climate that takes longer than 120 days to be ripe and ready to harvest.

to pick the adaptable ones. Catalogues are getting much better at explaining which veggies, fruit or herbs are suitable for containers or a tiny urban yard, but they still have a way to go. Some of their glowing descriptions are downright misleading for city gardeners.

Look for words in catalogue blurbs like "compact," "dwarf," "baby-sized," "climbing," "quick maturing" and "guaranteed to grow." And check out the container gardening section. Many catalogues now include one, because this method of growing things has taken the gardening world by storm.

With a limited space, skip those that grow very large or are sprawly. They'll prove annoying and or disappointing, for one reason or another. And when that happens, it's easy to get turned off gardening altogether.

Every veggie, herb and fruit included in this book I have personally tested. They can all be cultivated successfully in the city. However, their requirements for space and growing conditions vary a lot.

5 THINK TWICE BEFORE PLANTING THESE

Several well-known veggies have been deliberately omitted from this book. I recommend avoiding:

- **All members of the Brassica family.** These include broccoli, brussels sprouts, cabbage and cauliflower. Why? First off, they require a fair bit of space. More important, Brassicas are often attacked by two nasty little nuisances: the cabbage looper and cabbage worm. They look similar — wormlike — and are serious pests. In home gardens, they tend to appear out of nowhere.

Seeds or started plants?

The simplest and often best choice is to buy cell packs of started plants from a good garden center. They're usually cheap, easy to plant and reach maturity much faster than seeds — an important consideration in cool climates, where the growing season is short.

However, some veggies and herbs are best cultivated from seed because they either develop quickly and easily, or their seedlings are difficult to transplant. Don't bother to buy started plants of these. In all cases, seeds work just fine.

- beets
- carrots
- dill
- green beans
- peas
- salad greens
- soy beans
- summer savory
- summer squash

If you can install an inexpensive Gro-Light set-up or are blessed with a very sunny window-ledge, starting seeds early indoors is fun and a great antidote to long boring northern winters. Packets of seeds are, after all, dirt cheap, and you only need one packet each of things you want to grow. Another plus is that you get to start unusual varieties not sold at garden centers.

Try tomato and basil seeds first; they're among the easiest and most satisfying to grow from seed.

Using a sterile mix formulated for seed starting, plant seeds in any shallow container, keep the mix damp and covered with plastic wrap till, ah, that magic transformation — green fuzz — appears on the surface. Then, after the first two little leaves (called dicotyledons) develop, begin boosting seedlings once a week with a very mild solution of a water-soluble fertilizer such as 15-30-15. Within six weeks, you'll have strong, healthy tomato and basil plants, ready to put outside for the summer. Growing from scratch can be that simple.

(Commercially produced broccoli is doused more often with pesticides than any other crop in order to control them.) These critters chomp like crazy on beautiful, burgeoning heads of Brassicas and excrete horrid greenish goo all over them. If you garden organically, as most of us do now, it's a huge headache to banish them completely, because their eggs are laid in the soil and then keep reappearing every year. The best bet is to skip planting what they love to eat.

- **Corn on the cob.** Fresh-picked corn tastes like nothing else, no arguments about that. But it takes up barrow-loads of space. An even bigger drawback for urban gardeners is that corn is a magnet for raccoons and, to a lesser extent, deer. Both critters are becoming serious problems in many cities. Your neighbors will undoubtedly be happier if you bypass planting this taste treat of late summer and buy corn at the local farmers' market instead.
- **Fall and winter squash**. Acorn, buttercup, butternut, pepper, turban, delicata, hubbard, plus pumpkins, of course. There are many varieties to choose from, and most grow like gangbusters. They're also good winter keepers, and have great flavor. Only trouble is, these kinds of squash are, alas, space hoggers. Unless you have a huge area to let their vines ramble, or you can find a way to train them up a sturdy trellis, steer clear, because they are liable to strangle everything else in your little city garden.

6 PLANT THINGS PROPERLY — THEN BABY THEM A BIT

It's surprising how many people don't. Yet the fact is, you can't just shove seeds or started plants haphazardly into the ground and expect them to thrive on their own. They need lots of loving, particularly in the early stages. There's an old Chinese saying, "The best manure is the gardener's foot," and it's certainly true of growing our own food.

Get out there once a day (sometimes twice) at first, checking the progress of your plants. Be alert for too dry or too wet conditions, bug attacks, signs of

For decoration — or to eat?

Decide before you start. Many veggies, herbs and fruits can be combined successfully and beautifully with flowers and foliage plants in containers or small city gardens. In fact, this is a hot trend. However, if your intent is to grow food and wind up with a reasonably plentiful harvest, don't jam too many of both into a cramped space. The roots of veggies like tomatoes, bell peppers and celeriac need room to expand. You'll get better results with most edibles if they aren't forced to compete with other plants, particularly in containers.

Marigolds (the *Tagetes* kind) are one of the few flowers that I recommend interplanting with veggies (also edible nasturtiums, see page 80) because they give off a strong odor which seems to keep some bugs at bay. The presence of marigolds also encourages the development of beneficial nematodes in the soil. Buy started plants. They grow easily, don't take up much room and add a colorful touch to the garden or containers.

disease, weeds crowding out little seedlings and damage by birds, squirrels or nocturnal critters. As plants get established, they'll need less attention. But if you get them off to a good start early in the growing season, it will pay dividends at harvest time.

Important initial steps

- **Always read instructions on seed packets or labels** stuck into cell packs of started plants. The folks who write this information know their stuff. If the packet says "Barely cover seeds with soil," don't shove them deep into the ground. And if you're supposed to space bell pepper plants 12 in. / 30 cm apart, jamming a cell pack of six together into a small space isn't smart. It won't result in more peppers. The plants will just get spindly and sulk.
- **Remember adequate ventilation is very important in veggie gardens.** Give every plant room to catch the summer breeze and expand in a natural way. Then they'll be less prone to fungal diseases and bugs.
- **Water, water, water.** Veggie seedlings get thirsty more often in their early stages of growth than most ornamental plants. (Although beware of making them soggy.) They're also sensitive to cold. Don't splash icy water directly from the garden hose on to young leaves. Instead, keep a large plastic garbage bin close by and fill it daily

with water. Let the bin sit in the sunshine, warming up, then go around with a watering can when you get home from work. Water deeply around the base of plants, not with little dribbles. If you must water with a hose, do it in the morning, so plants can dry off during the day and not sit damp and shivering all night. (Would you want to sleep between clammy sheets?)
- **Weed, weed, weed.** It's tiresome, yes, yet our grandparents knew a thing or two when they toiled with hoes between the immaculate rows in their backyard plots. Veggies don't like competition. Although it's fashionable among modern eco-evangelists to insist that "every plant is a good plant" (and that leaving weeds is just fine, because they shade growing

crops from the sun), yanking the invaders out will result in sturdier, healthier plants. Do it early in the season. Once summer sets in, it is much harder — and hotter — to weed, because their roots are more firmly established. Never weed right after rain, either, when plants are soaked. This damages stems and leaves, inviting disease in. The same rule goes for dew-laden mornings. Wait till the sun has dried everything off before working in the garden. Early evening is best. It's also relaxing after a hard day at the office.

- **Mulch — up to a point.** We're all mulch maniacs now and a protective layer of something organic like leaves, straw or shredded bark around the base of plants certainly does help to keep moisture in and weeds out. But don't overdo it. During rainy summers, thick layers of mulch encourage slugs to multiply like

mad — and those slimeballs will creep out at night and chomp your precious veggies to shreds. Research at U.S. universities has also shown a huge jump in bacterial diseases triggered by over-zealous use of mulch. If the weather is wet for days on end, peel mulch back and let everything grow in bare soil. When it turns dry again, restore the mulch.

- **To fertilize or not to fertilize?** That depends. Some plants benefit from a boost, with others it's unnecessary and can even be harmful. Read instructions for each individual vegetable. I'm not a big fan of fertilizers in food gardens, partly because I'm too lazy to use them, but also because I prefer to enrich my soil with compost and manure beforehand. However, water soluble fertilizers are certainly a good idea at the seedling stage. (See Seeds or started plants on page 22.)

7 KEEP THOSE CRITTERS AWAY!

There are — sigh — more and more four-legged and two-legged nuisances in urban areas every day because cities provide animals, wild and domestic, with good pickings and safe places to roam. What to do?

- **Cats**. Stick bamboo barbecue skewers, pointed ends upward, closely together among plants. Try scattering orange peel, which they hate. Keep soil moist. Cats always prefer dry, dusty soil to scratch in.
- **Deer**. Oh dear, not much deters them. If you've planted a veggie garden near a ravine where Bambi and his buddies frolic, better move it elsewhere.
- **Rabbits, raccoons, skunks and squirrels**. Put cages (old wire shelves will do) around plants in the early stages. Try the bamboo skewer treatment. Get a dog or cat. However, the only thing that truly works is a garden hose equipped with sensors that trigger a blast of water when

the critters come within range. This may also work with deer. Just remember to turn the darn thing off during the day or you'll keep getting soaked yourself every time you go outside.

- **Pigeons, starlings and seagulls**. A problem on some balconies. Try stretching narrow black mesh netting over the entire balcony opening. (Netting also keeps birds away from ripening fruit.) A kid's wire Slinky toy stretched along railings may do the trick. Try shiny string, flapping bits of tin foil, or anything else that rattles. Forget plastic owls — they're ugly and don't scare anyone.

Don't use cayenne pepper. It may help a little, but is frowned upon by humane societies because critters get the powder in their eyes and can go blind. The same goes for urine of predators, which is often collected under inhumane conditions.

Bugs to banish

The insect world is huge. The more you grow things, the more you'll get accustomed to their presence in the garden. Many are beneficial, but watch out for these.

• **Aphids**. Can attack anything. Usually worse when plants are developing. So tiny, you often can't see them. Tell-tale signs: puckered-up or curled-under leaves, stunted or wilting plants, and (in heavy infestations) new shoots and buds covered in gucky blobs that may be whitish, orangey, greenish or black. Best remedy: blast aphids off with a strong jet from the garden hose, training it on the underside as well as tops of leaves, plus stems. Encourage ladybugs, which eat aphids. Alternative: spray with an insecticidal soap solution.
• **Caterpillars**. Unfortunately a real pest on the Brassica family of plants (like broccoli and cabbage): see page 22.
• **Cutworms**. Fat, cream-colored grubs, the larvae of a beautiful moth. They decapitate tomato plants at ground level. A problem in gardens, but not containers. Best remedy: push a matchstick (or twig) into the soil, so it touches tomato stems. Baffled cutworms won't saw through both.

Alternative: dig around before planting, remove cutworms and squash them.
• **Earwigs**.
Creepy crawlies that lurk under flowerpots and mulch, then emerge at night. Worse in wet summers. Tell-tale signs: chewed holes in leaves. Best remedy: remove places where they hide, that is, peel back mulch, tidy up garden debris, raise containers on legs. Alternative: scrunch up balls of damp newspaper in empty flowerpots, leave out overnight, dunk pots in a pail of soapy water the next morning. Dead earwigs will float.
• **Flea beetles**. Tiny insects that flit around, punching holes in leaves, particularly tomato plants. Best remedy: ignore them. They soon go away and do little damage.
• **Slugs**. Numero uno problem in veggie gardens, particularly when it's wet. Voracious, they multiply rapidly, skeletonizing plants and punching holes in everything, but particularly basil, leafy salad greens, tomatoes and peppers. Don't ignore slugs. Best remedy: remove places where they hide (mulch and lower leaves of plants.) Then handpick at night and squash. Alternative: spray with 1 tsp./ 5 mL ammonia mixed with water in a plastic spray bottle. Hit the slimeballs directly. Or saucers of beer, sunk at ground level. These must be

replenished every time it rains. Since beer is expensive, try 2 tbsp./30 mL brewers yeast mixed with 1 tbsp./ 15 mL sugar in a 2 cup / 500 mL yogurt container filled with water. Pour into saucers. The slimeballs crawl in, get drunk and drown.
• **Snails**. Same treatment as slugs.
• **Sowbugs**. Like little armadillos. Curl up when exposed to light. Mostly a nuisance in container gardens, hiding underneath pots, then tunneling their way up through the soil at night. They nibble on plants, then vanish the next day. Best remedy: check underneath flowerpots regularly. Stamp on sowbugs the moment you spot them, because they scatter like greased lightning.
• **Whitefly**. If clouds of little white insects ascend abruptly to the sky when you brush against plants, you have whitefly. They're common on tomatoes and herbs such as basil and not easy to get rid of. Try yellow sticky strips positioned close to plants. Be careful of bagged potting soil. Whitefly often gets into gardens via this route, because the winged hordes lay their eggs in it and then hatch out in spring.

What to do with herbs you bring indoors for the winter?

Easy. Give them a bath. This gets rid of the bugs and their eggs that may be lurking on the plant and in the soil.

The tropical herbs included in this book can all spend summer outside. But once fall frosts threaten, move them to warmer quarters indoors. Before this, on a sunny day, give each plant a drastic haircut, then dunk the whole thing, pot and all, in a big plastic container filled with lukewarm water and a few squirts of an insecticidal soap product. (Pure soap liquid works just as well and is usually cheaper. Don't use detergent.) Make sure the whole plant is immersed.

Leave for a few minutes, while bubbles rise. Then rinse pot and plant off in clean water. Let them dry out a little in the sun before coming inside. This is a chore, for sure, but is really worth the effort.

Diseases to deter

Four kinds of disease can affect veggies: cultural, fungal, bacterial and viral. It's a daunting list and the worst part is that most have no cure. All you can do is remove affected plants and throw them out. (But not in the compost!)

Disease tends to develop in too-damp conditions and when plants are packed too closely together. Be on the watch for these nasties:

• **Fusarium wilt**. Commonly known as damping-off disease. Mostly a problem when you start plants from seed (see page 24). A fungus develops at the base of seedlings, stems shrink inward and turn black. Then the hapless plant wilts and collapses. Remedy: yank out keeling-over plants the moment you see them. Even so, others

Diseases on tomato plants are usually triggered by weather conditions. Squashy patches like this are a tell-tale sign.

close by may succumb too. Buy seeds that are fusarium resistant. (They're marked "vf" on packets.)

• **Gray mold** (*Botrytis blight*). Fuzzy grayish patches appear in humid weather, particularly on squash foliage. They're

A straw mulch around the plants keeps moisture in and weeds out. But in too-wet conditions, thick layers of mulch encourage diseases to develop.

ugly but usually don't affect developing fruit. Remedy: cut off badly affected leaves if you can't stand looking at them. Otherwise ignore.

• **Powdery or downy mildew**. Similar to gray mold and equally unsightly. Remedy: spray with baking soda mixed in water if you have the energy. Cut off affected leaves. Otherwise ignore.

• **Late blight** (*Phytophthora infestans*). Common. Mostly hits tomatoes in wet summers, late in the season. Can be devastating, making fruit brown, squashy and inedible. A particular problem with heirloom kinds. See page 115. If you see black spots and curled-up leaves appearing on plants, cut the affected foliage off immediately and get rid of it in a sealed garbage bag so the spores won't spread.

A sudden storm can blow in remarkably quickly and wreck all your hard work in the garden.

If frosts come too early in fall, old cotton sheets are great for protecting ripening tomatoes at night.

8 PAY ATTENTION TO WEATHER FORECASTS

When growing food, you'd better find out what the experts are predicting in the next 24 hours because a sudden change in weather can break your heart. Ground frosts. Violent winds. Severe rain or hailstorms. The temperature soaring overnight. All of these can swoop in and destroy what you've been lovingly tending for weeks. And with climate change making its presence felt in many regions of the planet, such radical, unexpected shifts in weather patterns are becoming the norm.

Early in the growing season, check forecasts on radio, TV or government meteorological websites twice a day. (It's what farmers do.) If there's even a hint of late spring frosts on the way, cover up fledgling plants with light cotton sheets at night. Secondhand sheets are very cheap at thrift shops. Don't use plastic garbage bags, which won't stop freezing temperatures permeating through to the plants. Remove sheets in the morning, when the sun is up.

Throughout summer, be alert too, for strong winds and rainstorms. Secure plants to stakes or cover them with cardboard boxes, if necessary. And when fall rolls around, watch for Jack Frost to make a surprise return far earlier than expected — he often does. Protect ripening tomatoes from his frozen fingers using those cotton sheets again. Fail to treat him seriously and he'll turn luscious homegrown tomatoes into a squashy and disgusting mess overnight.

9 DON'T PLANT TOO MUCH

This is the biggest mistake beginners make, and it can turn growing food into a chore, not a pleasure. The fact is, most of us no longer have huge families to feed, so who needs to be saddled with two bushels of runner beans, massive mountains of tomatoes and dozens of those daunting zucchini torpedoes?

Be selective about what you grow. Plant a little of each veggie, herb or fruit at first. If you like these, put in more the following year. And after arriving home from the garden center with a six-pack of started pepper plants (they always seem to be sold that way) think seriously if you want, or have room, to grow six. It's so easy to fall into the trap of saying "Well, I may as well plant all this stuff, as I bought it." Yet what's far smarter is to share the excess starter plants with gardening buddies. That way, you don't wind up taking on a ton of labor that will inevitably become more and more tedious as the growing season wears on.

Thinking "small quantities, not big ones" is the way to make sure gardening stays exciting and fun. Try something new and different every year too. The novelty factor is important.

It's easy to go nuts at a garden center in spring. But in a small space, it pays to be choosy about what you grow.

10 DON'T EXPECT PERFECTION

We've all been conditioned to think that produce, whether it's veggies, fruit or herbs, has to look absolutely perfect. No blemishes. No bulgy bits. No nicks in the skin. Not even a suggestion of a nibble by some bug. Everything uniform size and squeaky clean — whether it's tomatoes, bunches of dill, or heads of lettuce.

Homegrown produce seldom looks like the stuff sold at the supermarket. But it usually tastes a heck of a lot better. (Right) Nothing is guaranteed to raise a smile quicker than a bowlful of yummy homegrown tomatoes, still warm from the sun.

Yet once we start gardening, it quickly becomes clear that Mother Nature isn't perfect. Not by a long shot. In fact she's often wilfully misshapen, covered in dirt and downright weird-looking. That means most home-grown food is unlikely to ever measure up in appearance to the offerings in supermarkets. But that's in its favor, really. It is scary how much commercially grown produce has to be manipulated and bullied in devastating ways nowadays in order to attain the fundamentally unnatural standards that consumers have come to expect.

And appearances aside, here's one exciting fact about growing your own. In almost every instance, the veggies and fruit you pick will be fresher, with much more honest-to-goodness flavor than supermarket produce. In fact, you won't quite believe anything could taste that delicious.

Asparagus Peas *Tetranogolobus purpureus*

Degree of difficulty
Easy in hot weather

Needs
Sun all day. Light soil

Where
In the ground or containers

When
Outside after soil has
warmed up

How
Seeds only. Grows quickly

Method
Plant several seeds 3/4 in./
1.9 cm deep. Thin when
plantlets are about 2 in./
5 cm high. Containers must
be at least 12 in./30 cm
wide

Problems
Rare

Harvest
When pods are
about 1 in/2.5 cm
long

Store
No. They don't keep
long

How much to grow
A couple of plants

This is perhaps the prettiest vegetable on the planet, perfect for containers on a sheltered, sunny deck. And it's so offbeat, visitors are sure to say "Wow. What's that?"

The plant produces thin, sprawly stems stippled with small leaves that fold up at night like wings. Its flowers are small too, but a knock-out wine red. Then the peas come along, frilled down the sides and fascinating to look at.

Some people say asparagus peas (also called winged beans) got their name because they taste like regular asparagus. Others argue that cooking requirements — they should be treated in the same way as their namesake — are the reason. Either way, they're a novelty and fun to eat, if you get to harvest a big enough crop.

Important things to remember

- Asparagus peas originated in scrubby wastelands of the Mediterranean and grow easily in hot, dry weather. But in cool summers, pea pods will be sparse.
- These are low-growing plants, which like to spread out. Space 3 ft./90 cm apart in the garden. If using containers, thin to only one plant per container. Their floppy stems can reach 3 ft./90 cm long, but don't try staking them because they're too numerous.

- Asparagus peas don't like competition. Keep weeds away in the garden by spreading a mulch of straw or shredded tree bark around the base of the plants.
- Pick peas when they're no more than 2 in. / 5 cm long. Do the "bend test." If they bend easily, they're edible. If they don't, they have probably grown too tough and fibrous to eat.

TASTE TREAT

Cooking asparagus peas

I think simple is best, because the flavor is subtle. Wash the pods. Prepare like green runner beans, topping and tailing them, then pulling off side strings (which become tough on older beans and should be removed).

Bring a few cups of water to a boil in saucepan. Drop the beans in, simmer for about 5 minutes. Drain well and serve with butter, salt and pepper. They are also surprisingly good mixed with a bit of cream and served on buttered toast.

Basil *Ocimum basilicum*

Degree of difficulty
Easy, but watch for bugs

Needs
Mostly sun. Afternoon shade good

Where
Preferably containers

How
Started plants easier. From seed, sow indoors four weeks before last frost. Don't move outside till weather warms up

Method
Seeds are like fly specks. Sprinkle only a smidgen of soil on top of soil. Tamp down, water. Thin seedlings. Don't crowd plants, or they may get black stem rot

Special requirements
Good, humusy soil or growing mix

Problems
Aphids, slugs, earwigs. Fusarium wilt (sometimes)

Harvest
Any time in summer. Snip leaves as needed

Store
No. Dried leaves lose flavor. Making pesto is better

How much to grow
Lots. At least six plants. Just about everyone loves basil

There's one big bugaboo with basil, which is now the most popular herb on the planet thanks to the universal appeal of Italian cuisine. We love it — but so, alas, do creepy crawlies.

Slugs and earwigs seem to appear magically whenever basil is around. So even though it's a good-natured plant that does well in the garden, use containers. That way, you can keep an eye on it.

Having had umpteen garden-grown basil plants chewed to shreds by the pesky critters, I now stick to pots placed up on my deck, with much better results. Aphids are also less bothersome there. (One tell-tale sign of aphids is wrinkled-up leaves. For remedies, see page 27.)

Important things to remember
- Keep nipping basil flower buds off. If you let them flower, leaves stop growing. Water often.
- This is a herb of lazy summer days. Don't bother bringing an established basil plant inside when fall comes. The stems get tough and woody, leaves become sparse. What's far more practical is to make pesto with the leaves earlier in the season. Scoop pesto into little jars and store them in the freezer. Or start new basil plants indoors in fall if you still have any energy left for gardening projects.

For fun
Mrs. Burns Lemon basil: Two great flavors in one, but leaves are unsatisfyingly small.
Lesbos basil (below): Greek, unique, very different. Traditional basil flavor plus strong hints of lemon and spices. Grows from cuttings only. Can reach 40 in. / 1 m high. Needs sun all day. Must be wintered over indoors.

TASTE TREAT

Chopping herbs is often a chore, but you can skip it with basil. Simply tear leaves into a salad. Or place whole small leaves on uncooked pizza, then add tomato sauce and cheese on top.

Recommended varieties
For Italian cuisine
Plain old Sweet basil: Oldie but goodie. Still one of the best.
Genovese basil from Italy: Largish, tasty leaves that don't turn black when you cut them.
Bush basil: Small leaves, best for drying, as they strip off the stems easily.
Green Globe: The biggest leaves. Great for tearing into pieces for salads.

For Thai and Vietnamese cuisine
Thai basil, **Spice basil** and **Siam Queen basil** all have a similar flavor —that is, classic basil with spicy overtones.

For decorative use
Magical Michael: Developed especially for containers. Forms shapely, pretty plant. Flavor is so-so.
Purple Ruffles: Probably the prettiest kind of basil. Great combined with any annual flowers.

Pole and Runner Beans
Phaseolus vulgaris

Degree of difficulty
Easy

Needs
Sun all day. Water regularly.

Where
Any place they can climb.
In the ground or containers

When
Spring, after soil has
warmed up

What
Seeds only. Started plants
may not take

How
Plant six seeds, thin to
two or three, spaced at
least 4 in. / 10 cm apart.
About 1 in. / 2.5 cm deep

Problems
Slugs and earwigs

Harvest
Before pods get big
and tough

Store
No. Won't keep long.
But they freeze well

How much to grow
Two or three vines — or
you'll get sick of eating
beans

Forget bush beans. Yes, our grandparents grew them, but they take up too much space and are a bore to pick. Squatting down and scrabbling around looking for ripe pods among a lot of leaves isn't fun on a hot day. (And you always miss a few, anyway.)

Also, slugs are a constant nuisance. Because bush beans grow close to the ground, the tender pods are all too easy for the slimeballs to reach and munch on.

So in small spaces, go for pole or runner beans instead. They're easy and fast, clambering quickly up trellises or fences and over ugly garages. On an apartment balcony, simply stretch a few pieces of string between you and your neighbor and, presto, you'll have a great temporary privacy screen for the summer.

And the best part: runner and pole beans grow too high off the ground for slugs to get at. They're also easy to pick. Their only real drawback is that they take longer (usually a week or two) to reach maturity than the bush kind. But trust me, it's worth the wait.

Important things to remember

- Pole beans do not require bees for pollination, so are best in wet summers with little sun. Runner beans look prettier and are more prolific, but you've got to have those insects buzzing about to get results. On highrise balconies, which bees find hard to reach, harvests of runners may be small.
- If it's wet and cold, whoa! Wait. Beans are incredibly touchy about low temperatures. The soil must be warm.
- They like good drainage, and a dollop of compost mixed into the ground or container. Some folks recommend fish emulsion (administered twice, at two-week intervals) in the initial stages, but my beans get no goosing from fertilizers at all and they do just fine.
- Don't plant them too closely together. The vines will behave like Boston Stranglers with each other and the end result will be fewer beans.

- Beans have an unfortunate habit of ripening all at once. So adhere to Commandment Number 9 of veggie gardening in the city (see page 31). Don't plant too many of them!

Recommended varieties

Runner Bean Wisley Magic: Absolutely my fave bean. Always grows, even in lousy weather. Pretty red flowers. Prolific. Longish green beans, full of flavor. Winner of the highest honor from the Royal Horticultural Society in the U.K.
Royal Burgundy: Popular. Widely grown. Prolific purple pods that are easy to spot among the leaves. Pods turn green during cooking.

TASTE TREAT

Tuscan bean soup

One of my faves, because lemon, basil and fresh beans are yummy together. You also don't have to make stock first.

- About 1 1/2 cups white kidney beans or navy beans
- 1 tbsp./15 mL each butter and olive oil
- 2 cloves crushed garlic
- 2 stalks celery, chopped
- 2 carrots
- A big scoop of pesto sauce (or 2 tsp./10 mL dried basil)
- 1 lb (about 3 cups) runner beans (fresh), cut in 1 in./2.5 cm lengths
- 1 large onion, chopped
- 3–4 tbsps. (45–60 mL) lemon juice (according to taste)
- About 5–6 cups (1.25–1.5 L) water
- Salt and pepper

Soak dried beans overnight, simmer in plenty of water till tender, about 1 hour. In a large, heavy saucepan, sauté onion, celery and carrots in butter and olive oil for a few minutes till they are well-coated, adding garlic at the last minute, so it doesn't burn. Add water and both kinds of beans, simmer gently for about half an hour, then add lemon juice and pesto or dried basil. Season to taste. (If pesto is store-bought, go easy on the salt.) Serve sprinkled with grated parmesan and chopped parsley.

Beets *Beta vulgaris*

Degree of difficulty
Easy

Needs
Mostly sun. Some shade okay

Where
In the ground or containers

When
Early spring, cool weather

How
Seeds or started plants

Method
Plant seed about
1/2 in. / 1.25 cm deep,
a finger-length apart.
Use containers at least
12 in. / 30 cm wide and
deep. Started plants should
be small. As they grow,
thin with nail scissors

Special requirements
Plenty of water, stone-free
soil

Problems
Slugs, earwigs (sometimes)

Harvest
Very early leaves for salads.
Beets when big enough
to eat

Store
No. Beets last only a week in
the fridge. Or pickle them

How much to grow
Half a dozen plants. Late
summer, plant more seeds,
if you have the energy

Love beets? Hate 'em? It seems there is no middle ground with this root vegetable. But if you're a fan, beets are great for urban gardeners because they adapt well to containers and look decorative. In fact, container-grown beets whose stems are a luscious crimson make good ornamental plants.

And besides classic purplish red, beets can be white like a turnip, gold, scarlet, blackish-red or even peppermint striped. Their shapes range from stubby and round to sausage-like.

Important things to remember

- If you want to eat home-grown beets, don't let the soil dry out. In containers, that means being vigilant with the watering can. Dried-out beets become hard and inedible.
- Small round varieties, not long cylindrical beets, are best for containers.
- Although beet greens are touted as delicious cooked or in salads, they're only worth eating when young. Don't bother after they grow more than 6 in. / 15 cm tall. The taste is bitter, the texture tough.
- Harvest beets when small. Tennis-ball-sized ones get hard, take ages to cook and are only suitable for winter soups. Grasp leaves in one hand and ease beets gently out of the ground, trying not to snap off the long root underneath.

- Keep this root intact and leave an inch or so of beet greens on top on when you boil them, or they will bleed and become anemic-looking and unappetizing.
- Beets go moldy quickly after cooking. Splash a bit of wine vinegar over them and they will keep much longer in the fridge.

Recommended varieties

Pablo: A baby beet from Europe. Good in containers, not much foliage and matures quickly.

Red Ace: Oldie but goodie. My favorite, because it's so dependable.

Chioggia: Italian heirloom variety. Hot with gourmets, wild striped flesh. Colors fade a lot when beets are boiled.

Roast beets with thyme, oregano and rosemary

It's customary to boil beets, but they are just as easy to roast and there's no stained saucepan to wash afterward. The taste is wonderful too. This recipe comes from gourmet cook Josephine Felton, who used to run a country hotel in Littledean, Gloucestershire, England.

- 3 large red onions
- 3 large beets (cooked or raw but not in vinegar)
- 1/2 cup / 110 g dark brown sugar
- 2 tsp. / 10 mL cumin seed
- 1/2 cup / 125 mL vegetable oil
- 2 crushed garlic cloves
- 1 tsp. / 5 mL each of fresh thyme, oregano and rosemary

Peel onions. Cut into sixths or eighths through the root so the layers stay together. Cut beets into similar-sized pieces. Put in roasting tin with other ingredients and mix well. Season with salt and pepper.

Cover with foil and bake at 350°F / 180°C for about an hour until veggies are softened. Remove foil. Bake 20 minutes more to caramelize the top.

Good eaten hot or cold as a salad. Serves 4 to 6.

Carrots *Daucus carota*

Degree of difficulty
Medium

Needs
Sun. Tolerates some shade

Where
Containers better than the garden, which must be deeply dug and free of stones

When
Spring. After frost, when soil is warm

How
Seeds only

Method
Sprinkle a smidgen of soil over seeds. Water regularly

Special requirements
Loose soil, not a rock anywhere

Problems
Carrot fly, maggots, slugs

Harvest
When you see well-formed carrots poking up

To store
A pail of damp sand. Stand carrots in it in a cool basement. They keep a couple of weeks in the fridge

How much to grow
A few as a treat, if storage facilities aren't available

Why bother with carrots? Well, the home-grown kind taste wonderful, far sweeter and less chewy than mass-produced ones at the supermarket. They're also fun.

Feathery carrot tops look as fetching as ferns developing in the garden. And pulling a fat, ripe carrot out of the soil, wiping it clean, then chomping on it, raw, surely ranks as one of veggie growing's most satisfying experiences.

Carrots are also great for containers, because you don't have to worry about getting rid of all the stones and rocks in the garden. (Leave these behind in the soil and you'll wind up with weird, misshapen carrots.) Just be sure to use a container at least 12 in. / 30 cm deep and pick a stubby variety.

Important things to remember

- Thin, thin, thin is the watchword with carrots. Carrot seeds are pinprick size, making it virtually impossible to space them evenly a planting time. As a result, too many little plantlets inevitably push up. These must be weeded out for the carrots to develop. Without thinning they'll be spindly and a fiddle to cook. Seed tape or pelleted seeds are easier than a packet of regular seeds, but more expensive.

- Soil should be loose. Add leaves or coir if it's clayey. But don't over-fertilize or add manure. Carrots will wind up covered in horrid, hairy roots if soil is too rich in nitrogen.
- Skip carrots described as being "long" or "tapering" in seed catalogues. They're elegant, for sure, but require perfect stone-free soil. Stubbies are more practical for home gardeners.

Recommended varieties

In the garden
Nantes: Blunt shape, very sweet.
Resistafly: Reputed to be good at repelling bugs.
Chantenay: Short, good in shallow, heavy soil.

In containers
Mignon: Matures quickly, sweet. Hassle free.
Thumbelina: Round, cute-looking, quite fast.

For fun
Purple Haze: Dark purple skin, orange interior. Kids love the lurid look.
Rainbow: White, yellow and orange carrots whose colors get brighter when cooked.

TASTE TREAT

Cumin carrot salad
- 6 large scraped carrots
- About 2 tbsp. / 25 mL chopped green onions
- 1–2 tbsp. / 15–25 mL white sugar (or according to taste)
- 1/2 tsp. / 2 mL salt
- 1 tsp. / 5 mL ground cumin
- 1 tbsp. / 15 mL fresh lemon juice
- Ground black pepper
- Chopped parsley

Grate carrots into a bowl. Combine everything else except parsley in a measuring cup, then mix into carrots and leave at room temperature for an hour or so. Sprinkle with parsley before serving.

Great for guests, because you can make this in advance. Keeps well in the fridge for a few days. And diet-conscious friends like this salad because it contains no fats.

Catnip *Nepeta cataria*

Degree of difficulty
Easy

Needs
Mostly sun. Light shade okay

Where
Preferably in the ground. Messy in containers

When
Outside in spring. A perennial, can stay outside year round

How
Seeds only. Grows quickly. Can be started indoors then moved outside

Method
Sow several seeds. Cover with smidgen of soil. Thin when 3 in. / 7.5 cm high

Problems
Rare

Harvest
Preferably before plants flower

Store
Yes. Dries well

How much to grow
One plant is ample

Ah, cats and catnip. My three kitties adore their daily "fix." On lazy summer mornings, they often head straight outside to chomp a stalk — or roll in the plant until they're blissed out and bug-eyed.

And I tolerate such behavior, because this wild herb is very easy to grow. Almost too easy. It's related to mint and once introduced into your garden, will drop seeds like crazy and keep popping up everywhere if you aren't vigilant.

However, that doesn't bother me at all, because I'm a catnip junkie too. It makes a soothing, sedative tea which I sip daily at bedtime. Vastly better, for sure, than popping sleeping pills with nasty side-effects.

Important things to remember
- If giving felines a treat is the objective, make sure to pick the right catnip — that is, the wild kind. There are several ornamental catnips around; one is called Faassens-*Nepeta x faassenii*. They are low-growing plants and make pretty groundcovers in gardens but are not a magnet for cats the way *N. cataria* is. Ask at garden centers if the catnip you're buying is the one your cats will like.

- Wild catnip grows up to 36 in. / 90 cm tall. Like a lot of uncultivated herbs, it's a dull-looking plant. If growing it in a container, keep cutting the stems back to prompt fresh green growth, which provides a more attractive appearance. (New leaves also taste best in tea.)
- To stop catnip spreading in the garden, cut off its white flowerheads promptly before they turn into tiny seeds. These are barely visible and will manage to drift everywhere.

Recommended variety

There is only one kind of wild catnip — *N. cataria*. But try an exciting relative, Lemon Catnip, *N. cataria ssp. citriodora* Lemony. Has a wonderful, strong smell of lemons, terrific in tea. Cats, however, prefer the plain stuff.

TASTE TREAT

Catnip tea

Cut a handful of fresh catnip leaves and stalks before they flower. Throw in a jug or teapot along with a stalk of Lemony Catnip. Pour on boiling water. Steep for 5 minutes. Serve with honey. A good night's sleep will surely follow.

Note: This tea can also be made with dried leaves and stalks during the winter, but may taste bitter. In that case, add more honey. Cats groove on catnip fresh or dried. Doling out a regular fix in the deep midwinter is a good way to stop them clawing the furniture.

Celeriac *Apium graveolens var. rapaceum*

Degree of difficulty
Easy

Needs
Mostly sun. Some shade okay

Where
In the ground or containers

When
Spring, after frost

How
Preferably started plants. Sow seeds indoors at least two months before last frost

Method
Mix in compost or well-rotted manure first. Space plants 12 in. / 30 cm apart in garden. Containers should be deep, at least 18 in. / 45 cm and 12 in. / 30 cm wide. Allocate only one plant per pot

Problems
Rare

Harvest
After a light frost in fall

Store
In a cool basement for several months. Cut off top leaves and roots or celeriac goes soft. Keeps a week or two in fridge

How much to grow
Lots, if you have storage facilities

Forget regular celery. It's a huge hassle to grow. But its rooty relative, celeriac, is a breeze and tastes virtually the same. This is in fact a very practical veggie for northern gardeners, because it stores well and is terrific in winter soups.

You can also grate the round, creamy-colored roots raw into salads (as the Swiss do), boil and mash them like potatoes, or dip thick slices in oil, then roast them in the oven. Young leaves snipped off the burgeoning plant impart a gentle celery flavor to salads or to a stock for soups. Don't use old ones, though, which turn awfully bitter.

Important things to remember

- Celeriac takes an eternity to develop — as long as 160 days. So started plants (if you can find them) are better than seeds, which may not mature before winter comes.
- As celeriac roots start swelling, they may stick up above the soil surface and turn green. This exposed part will become inedible, like potatoes that have been exposed to light. To turn the tops white again, scrunch up a layer of straw or leaves around the base of the plants.
- For salads, use young celeriac, that is, tennis-ball size. Big roots are tougher, but fine for soups.

TASTE TREAT

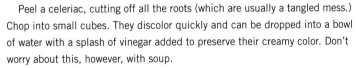

Celeriac soup

Don't let other veggies overpower the delicate flavor of celeriac. This recipe hits the right note.

Peel a celeriac, cutting off all the roots (which are usually a tangled mess.) Chop into small cubes. They discolor quickly and can be dropped into a bowl of water with a splash of vinegar added to preserve their creamy color. Don't worry about this, however, with soup.

Sauté with a medium-sized chopped onion in a saucepan containing a bit of olive oil or butter. Add about 4 cups / 1 L of vegetable or chicken stock and a bay leaf. Simmer for half an hour until the celeriac gets soft. (If it's a big root, this may take longer.) Remove bay leaf. Whir about half the soup in a blender, pour it back into the saucepan, add some chives and chopped fresh parsley (or sage), salt and pepper and cream (optional). Makes 4 servings.

Chard *Beta vulgaris*

Degree of difficulty
Easy

Needs
Mostly sun. Some shade okay

Where
In the ground or containers

When
Spring, after frost

How
Seeds. Started plants unnecessary, but use if you're in a hurry to harvest

Method
About 1/2 in. / 1.25 cm deep. In the ground, space seed about 12 in. / 30 cm apart. In a container, plant four seeds. Thin to one or two, depending on container size

Special requirements
Plenty of water

Problems
Slugs, earwigs (sometimes)

Harvest
When leaves look big enough to eat

Store
No. Keeps in fridge about a week

How much to grow
Two plants are plenty

Some people loathe chard, but that's undoubtedly because they've only ever eaten the supermarket kind. Often fibrous and too old (leaves should be picked young), it tastes bitter. Yet fresh from the garden, chard is something else: sort of like spinach, with stalks reminiscent of asparagus. Yum. I love it.

And chard (also known as Swiss chard) has two other pluses. Unlike spinach, it will grow easily in the garden or on a balcony in all kinds of weather and looks remarkably attractive. In fact, the chard varieties with brightly colored stalks make great decorative foliage plants.

Important things to remember

- Keep snipping off outer leaves when they're no more than 6 in. / 15 cms tall, leaving the "babies" at the heart of the plant intact.
- Chard becomes bitter if soil is too dry or leaves get oversized. To use in salads, pick very small.
- It can take a light frost in fall, but turns mushy if wintered over in the garden.

Recommended varieties

- **Bright Lights**: The trendiest kind. A rainbow of stalks in white, red, yellow, pink and orange. Beautiful in containers, but the colored stalks turn brown when cooked.
- **Container Pot of Gold** (left): Developed especially for urban spaces. Won't grow as big and overwhelming as regular chard. Lovely golden stalks.

Chard à la Aldona

This recipe comes from Aldona Satterthwaite, former editor of *Canadian Gardening*. She loves to cook, but like me, never measures ingredients precisely.

Finely chop 3 or 4 cloves garlic. Sauté in about 2 tbsp. / 25 mL of olive oil until just tender. Do not brown. Cut a big bunch of chard, rinse well, but don't whir in salad spinner. Trim off coarse ends and chop leaves and tender stems into smallish pieces (about 1/2 in. / 1.25 cm). Add to pan, sauté on gentle heat, covered, until leaves are tender, stirring occasionally — about 10 minutes.

The chard leaves will yield up water, which is good, because next you will whomp in as much blue cheese as you dare. Stir it in until a yummy sauce forms and coats the garlic and chard leaves. Taste for salt (likely unnecessary). Serve on cooked pasta with a generous grinding of pepper. Optional: add a splash of color with a handful of grape tomatoes on top, or maybe a bit of parsley.

Chives *Allium schoenoprasum*

Three cheers for chives. They're easy to grow, tolerant of most soils and look pretty, especially in early spring, when their little starry pink flowers seem to appear with lightning speed.

And snipping chive leaves into anything — soups, salad dressings, pasta dishes, cottage cheese, baked potato toppings — instantly gives the meal a touch of class.

The drawback to these boisterous members of the onion family is that they grow like gangbusters. By midsummer, a clump of chives often becomes a sprawly mess of long yellowing leaves and dried up detritus around the edge. This stuff is too tough to eat, and ugly to boot.

By all means grow chives — but use a firm hand. Let them know who's boss.

Important things to remember

- The roots of chives keep on spreading. If planted in the garden, dig up the clumps and divide them every three years.
- In containers, chive roots quickly expand to take up all the available space. Once this happens, snippable green leaves will diminish. Chives also crowd out other container-grown plants. So tip the pot out every spring or fall, cut a chunk of chive root off and replant it. (Give the remaining roots away to some unsuspecting newbie gardener.)
- Although chives flowers taste good (if you like things very oniony) and look decorative, remove them if you want leaves to keep on coming.
- Don't be afraid to whack back a chive clump by midsummer. Fresh green growth will soon appear.
- In fall, follow the example of German cooks, who dig up a chunk of chive root and bring it indoors, in a container. Stand this pot in good light, water regularly and you'll harvest fresh chives all winter. As a precaution, give the pot a bath — see page 28 — before it comes inside.

Recommended variety

- Garlic chives *Allium tuberosum*. Flat leaved. Not as bossy as regular chives. Flowers in late summer. A good bet for small gardens or containers, but has a stronger flavor which some people don't like.

Chive topping for taters

Get a handful of chives. The easiest way is to snip the long leaves off the plant with scissors. Wash under running water because they often pick up sand and bits of dirt. Pat dry in a tea towel. Then pick leaves over carefully, discarding tough ones and snipping off ends that are brown and dried up, because chives must be tender to taste good.

Chop leaves or snip them into small pieces with scissors, toss into a bowl of plain thick yogurt (not low fat) or sour cream, add 1 tsp. / 5 mL cumin or curry powder and fold in 1 tbsp. / 15 mL lemon juice. Don't add salt, which makes the mixture go watery. Leave to stand for an hour. Scoop onto hot baked spuds, fresh from the oven (to which you've added salt and pepper first).

Also delicious drizzled on to a salad of sliced tomatoes, cucumber and radishes. Don't keep this for more than a day or two in the fridge, though, as chives tend to get tough and stringy.

Cucumbers *Cucumis sativus*

Degree of difficulty
Easy

Needs
Sun all day

Where
In the ground or containers

When
After soil gets really warm

How
From seed. Plants mature quickly. Sow seed 1 in. / 2.5 cm deep

Method
Cukes like to climb. Provide supports within the container (obelisks, bamboo stakes, tree branches) or something on the wall behind

Special requirements
Warm weather. Water. Good growing mix

Problems
Cucumber beetles and viruses (sometimes)

Harvest
When cukes look big enough to eat

Store
Use up quickly. They don't keep well

How much to grow
Two plants

Farmers' markets are often crammed with cheap cukes in late summer. It's hardly surprising. They grow like mad if the weather's warm and suddenly, everyone's inundated.

So why bother with your own? Well, it's fun to watch them swelling on the vine. And they taste best picked and eaten the same day.

However, cucumber vines, which ramble everywhere, can present problems in tight spaces. Encourage them to grow up, not out, with a wall-mounted trellis or netting attached to stakes or a frame. The cukes will hang downwards and be straighter than on the ground.

Important things to remember
- Cukes need a very sunny spot and plenty of water.
- In a garden, keep the area around plants free of weeds. Or lay down black plastic, punch holes, sow seeds and let vines ramble over the plastic.
- Harvest early, not when they're old and huge, containing big bitter seeds.

Recommended varieties

Fanfare: Develops vines that are half the length of most cukes.
Container Bush Slicer: Compact variety (although it still prefers to climb up something).

For novelty
Lemon: Heirloom kind. Trendy. Oval, stubby fruits, lemony-colored. Very sweet, but takes ages to mature.
Armenian: Long and skinny, pale green, called "snake melon" in the Middle East. Vines grow very long.

TASTE TREAT

Cucumber raita

Great with spicy Indian dishes, as a sauce on baked potatoes, or for a salad on lettuce leaves.

Slice 2 small cucumbers (or one large) lengthwise, then into quarters. Cut out seeds, as many people find them hard to digest. If skins are tough, remove these too with a potato peeler before cutting cukes open. Dice the flesh. Combine in a bowl with a cupful of thick plain yogurt (not low fat), a mashed clove of garlic, 1 tbsp. / 15 mL lemon juice, a handful of chopped, fresh mint leaves and 1 tsp. / 5 mL of curry powder (optional). Vietnamese coriander (page 117) can be used instead of mint.

Let raita rest for an hour before serving, but don't keep it more than 24 hours. The cukes get watery and unappetizing.

Edamame / Soybeans *Glycine max*

Degree of difficulty
Easy in hot summers

Needs
Full sun. Moisture

Where
Garden or containers

When
Spring, after soil has
warmed up

How
Seeds only

Method
Work in compost or
composted manure first.
In containers, use good
potting soil. Plant 1/2 in./
2.5 cm deep, about a
finger-length apart

Problems
Aphids sometimes

Harvest
When pods are plump
but not splitting apart

Store
Yes, beans can be shelled
and dried. But freezing
whole pods is less hassle

How much to grow
A few to try. If you like
them, plant more

Edamame (the Japanese name for a certain type of soybean) is all the rage as a cocktail snack. And it is certainly a novelty. The beans have a nutty flavor, unlike the standard soapy-tasting soybeans sold in bulk at health food stores.

They can be served warm, cold or after roasting in the oven. What's fun is to crack the whole pods open with your teeth to get the beans out. Kids love doing this — so serve them edamame (pronounced Ed-a-marm-may) often because soy is loaded with protein for growing bodies, yet contains virtually no fat.

Frozen bags of pods, imported from China, are what most fans go for. Each little pod contains two or three beans. Yet cultivating your own isn't complicated. This is also a veggie that adapts well to containers and looks quite decorative.

Important things to remember

- Seeds will rot in cold, wet ground. Wait till all frosts are past. In poor, clayey soil, put a scoop of mycorrhizal fungi (sold at garden centers, usually under the brand name Myke) into planting holes. This helps the plant take up nitrogen from the soil.
- Watch for aphids. One telltale sign is leaves puckering up and turning yellow. Douse plants in an insecticidal soap bath (see page 28) if infestations are serious. Encourage ladybirds, which eat aphids.
- Plants sprout quickly. They can grow bushy and reach up to 36 in. / 90 cm high but are usually smaller. Several per container is fine, but don't jam them in. Also, don't make them compete with other plants.
- The beans mature quickly in hot sunny summers. Regular watering boosts their sugar content. In prolonged rainy spells, they take longer to mature.
- Pods are covered in odd, fuzzy hairs. They're ready to pick when still green. Don't wait until they turn beige and start to split open.

How to cook and serve edamame

Wash about 4 cups of edamame pods.
Don't shell them. Boil 6 cups / 1.5 L of water
in a large saucepan. Add 1/2 tsp. / 2 mL salt, throw pods
in, and return to boil. Cover and cook for about 6 minutes,
no longer. Drain.

Serve warm or cold as is. Simply peel or crack pods open
(it is easier when they are warm). Pods can also be roasted
in a 350°F / 180°C oven for about 20 minutes. The taste
is nuttier. Drizzle them with a bit of olive oil before cooking,
plus salt and pepper. Cool then serve. Great with beer.

Eggplant/Aubergine *Solanum melongena*

Hate eggplant? This veggie, also known as aubergine, certainly inspires strong sentiments. But even if you detest it, cultivate a couple of plants anyway, because eggplant looks really cool growing in a container.

The shapely gray green leaves are fun to stroke. Delicate violet flowers come next. Then there's the fascinating pendulous fruit, shiny as patent leather shoes, in a glorious purple. (Also plum, striped color combinations and ivory white.) What more could anyone want in a container plant for a deck or balcony?

Important things to remember

- Eggplant, originally from India, must have heat and sunshine. It will languish in cool, rainy summers.
- Temperature is crucial. If nights are cool, flowers fall off and there will be no fruit. Keeping the container beside a south-facing wall which retains heat at night is good.
- Container-growing works better than the ground, because you can bring the pot indoors on unseasonably chilly nights.
- Allow no more than five fruit per plant — you'll usually get less than that anyway. If there are lots of flowers, pinch a few out. The remaining eggplants will develop better.

Recommended varieties
- **Little Prince**: Great in containers. Small, oval fruits.
- **Fairy Tale**: An award-winning variety developed for containers. Purple and white. Fruits early.

Grilled Italian eggplant sandwich

Cut eggplant in thick slices. Sauté in olive oil that's hot. (It will soak up too much oil if the frying pan is too cool.) Drain on paper towels. Place eggplant slices on a French baguette slit lengthwise. Add thinly sliced mozzarella on top. Smear on some pesto, then top it with slices of tomato, plus salt and pepper. Finish with another layer of sautéed eggplant, then the other half of the baguette.

Squash the whole thing down with the palm of your hand, then zap in the microwave for about 25 seconds, till cheese has melted. Or, if you have time (and don't like soggy, microwaved bread), wrap the sandwich in tin foil and cook in a preheated 375°F / 190°C oven for about 10 minutes.

Epazote *Dysphania ambrosioides*

Degree of difficulty
Easy

Needs
Sun. Some shade okay

Where
In the ground or a container

When to plant
Spring

How
Seeds or started plant

Method
Cover seeds with a smidgen of soil. Started plants require no special treatment in the garden. A light growing mix in a container is best

Problems
Rare

Harvest
Snip sprigs as needed

Store
Yes. Can be dried

How much to grow
One plant. A little goes a long way

Epazote smells weird. Modern cookbooks describe it in polite terms as "musty" or "pungent." But to me, it's more like paint thinner.

The Aztec description was equally unflattering. The word "epazote" comes from two words, *epatl* and *zotl*, which in the Nahuatl language mean "smelly animal."

Yet stinky or not, if you want to impart an authentic flavor to any Mexican bean dish, skip cilantro and use this instead — because oddly enough, epazote tastes terrific in spite of that smell.

This herb serves a practical purpose too. It is believed to get rid of the gas associated with eating beans and may dispel the gut-wrenching intestinal parasites that are common in the tropics.

Important things to remember
- Epazote is easy — almost too easy — to grow, even in northern climates. A lone seed will quickly develop into a weedy, bushy and rather ugly plant. If your space is limited, keep it confined to a container.
- Flowers are so small, you'll hardly notice them. Then, right afterward, dozens of ball-like seeds will appear very rapidly, arranged in rows down the stems.
- Leaves are best for cooking, so it's important to keep trimming the plant to stop this flowering process happening.
- For winter use, dry the leaves. (Most epazote in Mexico is sold dried.) The plant can be left outside year round, but in northern climates, put a protective mulch over it in the fall.

Black beans with epazote

- 3 cups beans, washed and picked over
- Water to soak
- 1 tbsp. / 15 mL canola or corn oil
- 1 chopped onion
- 4 garlic cloves, crushed and chopped up
- 2 or 3 sprigs of epazote
- Salt to taste

Soak beans overnight. Simmer in lots of water till they start to go soft. (This can take several hours, as black beans require longer to cook than other dried beans.) Heat oil in Dutch oven, add onion, stir till transparent, add half the garlic, then beans. Cover with water (save it from the beans), simmer for about half an hour, add chopped epazote and the rest of the garlic. Simmer another half an hour, till thick and fragrant. Let this dish sit overnight for best flavor.

Serve it with salsa verde (page 111), some grated Monterey Jack or cheddar, and corn tortillas or chips.

Fava Beans *Vicia faba*

Degree of difficulty
Can be tricky

Needs
Cool weather

Where
In the ground or containers

When
Early spring, before weather heats up

What
Seeds or started plants (if you can find them)

How
Space about 1 foot /
30 cm apart. In containers, only one plant per pot. Plant seeds about 1/2 in. /
1.25 cm deep

Problems
Aphids

Harvest
When pods are about
6 in. / 15 cm long

Store
No. But shelled beans can be frozen

How much to grow
Two plants. More if you love the taste

Favas? Most of us are familiar with them as flat, dried beans, oval-shaped, sold in health food stores. (You can also find canned favas, but don't bother. The taste is sour and unpleasant.)

Yet fresh favas are something else: delicious, unique, unlike any other bean. And they are great fun to grow.

Known as broad beans in the U.K., where people love them, favas look rather retro, with greenish-gray leaves which unfold like pleated skirts and unusual black and white flowers. The bean pods are big, fat and bright green, with a weird growth habit: they start at the bottom of the plant's stem and work their way up.

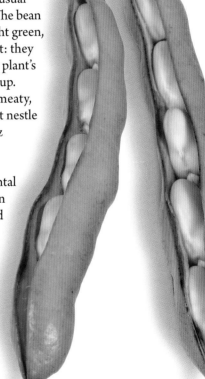

The edible part is the meaty, greenish-white beans that nestle in soft white, pillowy fuzz within the pods.

I actually find favas as attractive as any ornamental foliage plant. Grow one in a container on a deck and people will say: "Wow. What's that thing?"

Be sure to recycle discarded bean pods in the compost, as they are a great source of nitrogen.

Important things to remember

- Favas only do well in cool summers. If the temperature soars, forget it.
- In the right conditions, plants may grow tall. Average height in northern climates is about 18 in./45 cm high.
- They are prone to aphids, which cling in thick black gobs to stems and emerging leaves and prevent flowers and pods from forming. Blast them off with a jet of water from the garden hose as soon as you notice an aphid attack.
- Don't wait to harvest the pods until they develop brown blemishes and cracks down their seams. Pick while the beans are young and tender.

TASTE TREAT

Cooking fava beans

Split open pods lengthwise by running a kitchen knife down the seams. Remove beans, checking for blemishes and bugs (although there aren't usually any). Drop into boiling water for about 5 minutes. Don't overcook. Drain and serve warm with butter, salt and pepper.

The herb summer savory is a good accompaniment to favas. They are also delicious mixed with a vinaigrette and served cold.

Garlic *Allium sativum*

Degree of difficulty
Surprisingly easy

Needs
Mostly sun. Some shade okay

Where
In the ground. May not survive in containers

When
Fall

From seed
No

How
Make small holes. Drop individual cloves in, pointed side up, about 2 in. / 5 cm deep, a hand-span apart

Problems
Rare

Harvest
When top leaves go brown and floppy. Dry in sun, then bring indoors

Store
Yes. In dark, dry cool place, not the fridge

How much to grow
A planted clove yields one garlic bulb. A dozen or so bulbs last a couple of months in my kitchen

To the French, it's *ail*. Italians say *aglio*. In Mexico, the moniker is *ajo* (pronounced aho). Whatever way you say it, garlic is one smelly yet sensational seasoning, popular the world over.

There are two kinds: hard-neck has a central stiff stem and stores well. Soft-neck, mostly sold in supermarkets, won't keep as long. Note: Big fat elephant garlic isn't really garlic at all, but a type of leek.

Garlic is truly easy to grow. Just bury the cloves in the ground in fall, spread a mulch of leaves or straw over the whole area, then ignore all winter. In spring, pull the mulch off and green shoots will pop up quickly. Then come August, dig up the swollen garlic bulbs from the soil and prepare to be popular. (My garlic always seems to grow fatter, with far more flavor, than the stuff sold in supermarkets. Friends always clamor for it.)

In fact, there's only one drawback to growing garlic: like homemade compost, you'll never have enough.

Important things to remember

- Plant cloves anytime in fall, before freeze-up. Garlic likes good soil, enriched with compost or manure. If your garlic bulbs are small (a common complaint), beef up the nutrient content in your soil.
- Skip supermarket garlic for planting. It mostly comes from China or California.
- Seek out locally grown seed garlic — tougher, more suited to your climate and less prone to the only nasties which may attack garlic — stem and bulb nematodes. Look for seed garlic in farmers' markets and at garlic festivals in early fall.
- Pick full, heavy bulbs, not dried-up ones. Pry bulbs apart carefully when you plant. Broken or split cloves won't grow.
- Give garlic room. You can certainly plant cloves at random in the garden as critter deterrents (gardeners discovered long ago that squirrels hate garlic) but the stuff destined for the kitchen will develop better without competition.
- If you're trying garlic in a container, it must be deep and have sides lined with Styrofoam. Plant only three cloves in the center of the container (deeper than if you're growing it in the ground), then wind bubble wrap around and over the container top. A protected spot is good. So is an area where the container will get covered in snow, as the white stuff acts as a good insulator.
- In mid-June, early July, cut all the scapes off. These are the twirly "pigtails" that shoot up from the center of the plant and contain new flowerheads. Leave these on and your bulbs in the soil below won't develop as well.
- Fertilizing isn't necessary, but weeding is. Keep the area around garlic plants clear.
- Don't wait too long to harvest. Bulbs should be intact. When their papery skins start to split apart, they won't keep long.
- To avoid bulb and stem nematodes (for which there is no remedy — the crop must be destroyed), try not to grow garlic in the same location year after year. Rotating everything in the vegetable garden is best.

Ground Cherries *Physalis peruviana*

Degree of difficulty
Relatively easy

Needs
Sun all day, warm
temperatures

Where
In the ground or wide
containers

When
Spring, after frost

How
Started plants are best,
if you can find them.
From seed, start indoors
six weeks before last frost

Method
Don't stake, even
though they grow up to
3 ft. / 90 cm tall and
sprawl everywhere

Problems
Rare, because husks
protect fruit

Harvest
Before frost, when husks
look fully developed

Store
Fruits keep about six
weeks in a cool dry place

How much to grow
Two plants

Ground cherries are cousins of trendy tomatillos and have been around a long time. Their taste is often described as a cross between cherries and kiwi fruit, with a touch of tomato.

They are most often used to garnish plates of hors d'oeuvres in restaurants, because the orangey-hued fruits look very decorative when their outer husks are peeled back. Yet in bygone days, ground cherries were a favorite in pies. Cultivate them in the same way as tomatillos (page 110).

But be warned: Once introduced into a garden, ground cherries self-seed everywhere and tend to stick around forever!

Recommended variety
Aunt Molly: From Poland, does well in cool climates.

Ground Cherry Pie

- A frozen pie shell
- About 3 cups of ground cherries, husks removed
- 2/3 cup / 125 g white sugar
- 2 tbsp. / 25 mL water
- 2 1/2 tbsp. / 15 g flour

Preheat oven to 425°F / 220°C. Do not thaw out pie shell. Mix cherries, sugar, water, and flour in a bowl. Pour into pie crust.

Bake for 20 minutes at 425°F / 220°C. Then lower temperature to 300°F / 160°C. Bake 30 minutes more, until filling is set. Cool before serving.

Alternatively, make small tarts with this mixture in individual frozen pie shells, but reduce the cooking time.

Lettuce *Lactuca sativa*

Degree of difficulty
Mostly easy

Needs
Cool weather

Where
In the ground or containers; shallow containers are fine

When
Spring, after frost

How
Seeds. Started plants unnecessary, as plants mature quickly

Method
Space seed about 1/2 in. / 1.25 cm apart. Sprinkle a smidgen of soil on top. Pat down and water. Thin as plants develop

Special requirements
Cool, moist soil. Heatwaves make plants "bolt" (start flowering and turn bitter)

Problems
Slugs, earwigs. Sometimes aphids

Harvest
Often in three or four weeks

Store
No. Greens keep only a few days in the fridge

How much to grow
Half a dozen plants. Plant more later on

Once, you could find only one kind of lettuce: boring and tasteless iceberg, which had little nutritional value. But not anymore. Now, there's a wide choice — traditional head lettuce, like iceberg, plus romaine, butterhead, Bibb, leaf lettuce, red lettuce and some super mixes (see page 74).

Most are easy to grow. All they require is a cool spring and reasonably good soil. And they're worth growing because there's nothing quite like snipping fixings for a salad from your own garden. Do it early in the morning, when the dew's still on the leaves. The flavor and freshness beat any salad greens sold at the supermarket.

Important things to remember

- Don't let soil surrounding lettuce completely dry out. It must be kept steadily moist, but not soggy.
- Leaf lettuce is simpler to grow than classic head lettuce, because you snip off the leaves as you need them. There's no waiting around for the head to mature. (Also, heads often split in changeable weather.)
- Harvest leaves off all lettuce plants from the outside, leaving the center intact.
- Slugs or earwigs are always lurking somewhere! Before eating, soak greens in a sinkful of water with a tablespoon of salt added. Leave for half an hour only, as longer will turn leaves mushy. This bath makes creepy crawlies float to the surface — thankfully, dead.

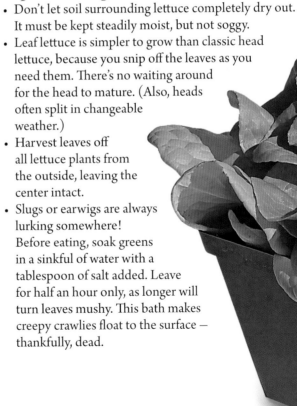

Recommended varieties

- **Tom Thumb lettuce (also called Garden Babies Butterhead)** (below): Developed especially for small urban gardens. Petite, round lettuce heads in bright green that do well in containers and look attractive. Try an ornamental row of three in individual containers on a deck.

- **Leaf lettuce mixtures**: Usually contain several kinds of lettuce, some frilly, some plain and in different colors, like bronzy red and purple. They are easy to snip off for use in salads.
- **Freckles**: A novelty heirloom lettuce, speckled with red. Less inclined to bolt in warm weather than other kinds. Fun if you like something different.

Lime Balm *Melissa officinalis*

Degree of difficulty
Easy

Needs
Mostly sun. Some shade okay

Where
In a container. May not survive outside in cold areas

When
Year round

How
Started plant. Seeds take too long

Problems
Rare

Harvest
Snip off fresh leaves. Use in cooking and herbal teas

Store
No. Dried leaves lose their flavor

How much to grow
One pot is ample

A h, luscious limes. Their tropical fragrance, more powerful than lemons, always transports me straight back to the Caribbean, where I lived as a teenager.

And with this herbal version, you can keep the scent on hand year round. Lime balm is a relative of more widely grown lemon balm, but I find it superior to the lemon-scented kind for two reasons. First, the fragrance is crisper and more pronounced. Second, the plant won't become a nuisance, spreading everywhere in the garden, as lemon balm often does.

Like many herbs, it's not a particularly decorative plant, although the leaves are a nice, bright shade of green. In milder areas, you can plant it in the ground and leave it as is. But if you experience severe winters, treat this one as a potted plant.

Important things to remember

- Like most culinary herbs, lime balm gets straggly when there's not enough light. It needs a sunny spot inside or out. Keep pinching new buds back to stop the plant flowering if you want to use the leaves in cooking.
- If container grown, bring the pot back indoors before frost hits.
- In preparation for its winter quarters, give the plant a drastic haircut. Then treat it to a soap and water bath (see page 28) to kill nasties lurking in the soil.
- Leaves going brown, particularly around the edges, mean lime balm needs more water.

TASTE TREAT

Lime balm guacamole

This is a variation on a recipe devised in the kitchens of the Royal York Hotel, a Toronto landmark which is fortunate to have a lovely rooftop herb garden. Hotel chefs use lemon balm, but it's delicious with lime balm too.

- 3 avocados, pitted and peeled
- 2 green onions, trimmed and sliced
- 1 minced garlic clove
- 2 tbsp. / 25 mL lime juice
- 2 small plum tomatoes, de-pipped and chopped small
- 1 small handful lime balm leaves, stems removed
- 1/8 tsp. / .5 mL cayenne pepper or hot sauce
- Salt to taste

Place the avocados in a bowl and mash with a fork or potato masher to a coarse puree. Add green onions, garlic, lime balm and stir into the guacamole mixture. Season with the pepper and salt.

Try this smeared in a chicken sandwich or on top of smoked salmon. It's also good as a dip for tortilla chips.

Melons *Cucumis melo*

Degree of difficulty
Easy if summer's warm

Needs
Sun all day

Where
Preferably in the ground.
If container grown, vines
need support

When
Spring after frost

How
Started plants easiest

Method
With seeds, make a
mound of compost. Plant
six seeds 1 in. / 2.5 cm
deep. Thin to two seedlings,
a hand-span apart. Use
same depth with containers
and provide a trellis

Problems
Slugs in wet weather

Harvest
When you prod fruit with
a finger and it no longer
feels hard

Store
No. They keep only a
couple of weeks

How much to grow
Two vines ample

Marvelous melons. Refreshing and low calorie on a hot day. And while most of them come from warm climates, they can be surprisingly easy to grow during northern summers. The trick is to pick short-season varieties that don't take an eternity to ripen.

Garden melons often wind up smaller than the large, commercially grown ones sold at the supermarket. But their flesh is usually superior — sweet, juicy, and with a texture that doesn't feel like a turnip when you bite into it.

Cantaloupes and musk melons are the best kinds to try. Forget watermelons: they will sulk unless the summer is very hot. The same goes for honeydew melons.

Important things to remember

- Don't plant seeds or started plants until the temperature reaches about 70°F / 20°C during the day.
- Heat and sun are vital. The best (and easiest) way to grow melons is to pick a south-facing spot, lay down a large sheet of black plastic over the soil, then cut a hole about 12 in. / 30 cm across. Add a scoop of compost, push in started plants or seeds and cover them with only a bit of soil. Let vines ramble over the plastic.

- In a small space, make your melons grow up. A sunny wall or fence is good. Provide strings or a trellis for the long, straggly vines. Support developing fruit with old onion bags tied to the supports.
- If melons aren't quite ripe when fall frosts arrive (which often happens), throw a cotton sheet — not plastic — over them for the night, then remove it in the morning, once the sun is up.

Recommended varieties
Alaska Muskmelon: Oval-shaped, sweet, tasty. Usually matures in 75 to 80 days.
Earlisweet Muskmelon: Small, round fruits. Dependable and delicious.
Minnesota Midget: Another round variety. Dependable. Developed especially for cool climates.

Note: Ask at a neighborhood garden center about local melons. There are often varieties available that have been handed down by generations of gardeners (and farmers) who live in the area. These will be particularly suited to your growing conditions.

Old onion bags are great for supporting melons grown on a trellis.

Mesclun Mix

Salad fixings have come a long way, baby. Once, it was customary to pull apart a head of lettuce (usually iceberg), quarter a few tomatoes and throw them into a bowl. That constituted a salad. But nowadays, gourmet cooks are opting for much more exciting ingredients. Leading the pack of possibilities are what are known as mesclun mixes. The name (which is pronounced Mez-CLUN, not mescalin) comes from a dialect spoken in the south of France and signifies immature greens, picked young.

These greens, now sold bagged in most supermarkets, are very easy to grow yourself. A typical mix may contain arugula, beet leaves, winter kale, mustard and radish greens, plus several kinds of lettuce, chicory and endive.

Important things to remember

- Mesclun mixes must be picked when the leaves are very small. Leave them to grow too big and some ingredients, particularly endive and chicory, will taste so horribly bitter, you'll gag.
- Most kinds are ready for picking in a remarkably short time. Don't delay. They will produce flowers and go to seed in a flash when your back is turned. Once that happens, they are inedible.
- Always keep mesclun mixes well watered. This is particularly important if you're growing them in containers.

- Cut leaves about 2 in. / 5 cm above the soil surface, in order not to injure the plants and to keep more leaves coming along.

Recommended varieties

- **Provencal Winter Mix**: A famous mesclun mix from a trendy part of France. Includes three kinds of lettuce, roquette, corn salad, radicchio, endive, parsley and chervil.
- **Mild Mesclun Mix**: If you don't like spicy or sharp-tasting greens, this is the one to try. Contains several kinds of lettuce, plus Chinese greens such as Pak Choi and kale.

- **Herby Salad Mix**: A range of tastes, colors and textures, including lettuce, Mizuna, rocket, Greek cress, giant red mustard and chicory.

For more growing instructions, see Lettuce on page 68.

Mint *Mentha spicata*

Degree of difficulty
Almost too easy

Needs
Sun or partial sun.
Tolerates some shade

Where
In the ground or a container

When
Perennial. Stays outside
year round

How
Buy a started plant.
Seeds take too long

Method
Average soil fine

Problems
Rare. Leaves sometimes
get rust

Harvest
After a few weeks. Mint
shoots up quickly in spring

Store
No. Dried mint is
flavorless. Chopped fresh
leaves can be frozen
in ice cube trays

How much to grow
One plant, with caution!
Mint grows like mad

The range of mints available nowadays is staggering. There's chocolate mint, banana mint, apple mint, grapefruit mint, wintergreen mint, pink candypops mint…. The list goes on and on. A few kinds have become hot items for use in cocktails (see Mojito Mint, page 78).

However, the most common kind, spearmint (also called garden mint), is still probably the best for cooking, because it has a sweet, pronounced flavor that's instantly recognizable. It's also a no-brainer, seldom bothered by bugs or diseases, and winters over outside with no hassles.

Important things to remember

- Mints grow on runners that fan out below the soil surface. Spearmint is one of the quickest to get out of control, spreading everywhere.
- In a small garden, confine the plant to a large metal bucket, filled with soil and sunk to soil level. Make a couple of drainage holes in the bottom of the bucket. Every couple of years, dig up the bucket and divide the roots, otherwise the plant will become too dense to grow well.
- Once mint flowers, it stops producing fresh, tender leaves. Snip the stem tops off regularly to keep new foliage coming.

TASTE TREAT

Chick pea dip with mint

This recipe is my own invention and always gets rave reviews at parties. Dried chickpeas, not canned ones, are best. Be generous with the mint, which must be fresh.

- 3 cups chickpeas, soaked overnight then boiled till soft
- About 1 cup / 250 mL good olive oil
- 1/2 cup / 125 mL lemon juice (more if you like a piquant flavor)
- 4 to 5 large cloves garlic, chopped
- Big handful of mint, stems removed (or more to taste) then roughly chopped
- A few shots of piri-piri, a Portuguese hot sauce
- Salt to taste
- Paprika

Whirl half the garlic, lemon juice, oil and mint together in blender. Throw in half the chick peas, whirl again to turn to a thick puree. Repeat procedure with rest of ingredients. Tip the lot into a bowl. Fold in salt and piri-piri. Scoop into small dipping dishes, sprinkle with paprika. Garnish with a mint sprig. Serve with fresh radishes, carrot and celery sticks.

Note: This recipe makes lots of dip. It lasts about a week in the fridge and is also delicious with cheese and tomato slices in pita bread. Freeze the excess. It lasts well but may be a bit runny when thawed.

Mojito Mint *Mentha x villosa*

Degree of difficulty
Easy

Needs
Sun. Tolerates some shade

Where
In the ground or container

When
Spring. After frost

How
Started plant only

Method
Average soil, but keep watered. Outside, mulch in winter. Container-grown, bring indoors in fall

Problems
Rare

Harvest
Snip leaves regularly

Store
No. Chopped fresh leaves can be frozen in ice cube trays, but lose flavor quickly

How much to grow
One plant

A h, mouth-smacking mojitos. How to make them taste exactly right? With this herb, amigos.

Mojito mint is the crucial ingredient in Cuba's famous cocktail, the mojito, which writer Ernest Hemingway sipped back in his Havana days. It's now enjoying a rebirth, thanks to James Bond, who drank one in the movie *Die Another Day*, starring Daniel Craig.

Its homeland is the tropical island of Cuba. The leaves are bright green and crinkly, the stems an attractive purplish-red. And the flavor is different from regular garden mint — softer, mellower, not as sweet. What's really surprising is that northern gardeners can grow this plant successfully. Simply treat it like any other mint in the garden. However, if you live in a very cold area, give it a protective mulch in winter.

Important things to remember

- Mints spread on runners that fan out below the soil surface and can get out of control. See notes on other mints on page 76.
- To keep fresh leaves coming for cocktail hour, pinch out new shoots, so the plant grows bushy.
  If grown in a container, cut it back hard before bringing indoors in fall.
- Can't find mojito mint? Plain old spearmint will suffice in a pinch. But try Mexican margarita mint (preceding page), which has strong hints of lime and marries nicely with the other flavors.

Hemingway's Mojito

This recipe comes from Conrad Richter, boss of internationally known Richter's Herbs in Uxbridge, Canada. Richter received a cutting of mojito mint from a visitor to Cuba, Catherine Naismith, and was the first grower to start propagating this herb successfully in North America.

- 1/2 to 2 tsp. / 2–5 mL sugar (depending on taste)
- 1 large sprig mojito mint
- 1 ounce white rum
- 1 ounce lime juice
- Ice
- Soda water

Spoon sugar into glass, add mint sprig. Pound both with a flat instrument or a pestle to crush the mint into the sugar. This is called "muddling" and releases the oils. Add ice, rum, lime juice. Fill with soda water and stir.

Nasturtiums *Tropaeolum majus*

Degree of difficulty
Easy

Needs
Full sun. Poor soil

Where
In the garden. Even better in containers

When
Spring, after frosts finish

How
Seeds best. Started plants difficult

Method
Just cover seeds with a smidgen of soil. If starting indoors, use peat pots. Do not fertilize or plant in rich soil

Problems
Slugs, earwigs, sometimes aphids

Harvest
Cut fresh leaves and flowers anytime. For seeds, wait till they start turning a beige color

Store
Seeds can be dried. Or pickle them

How much to grow
Lots. Use them to prettify your pots of veggies!

Edible flowers aren't my thing. I'd rather have them looking lovely in the garden. There are so many wonderful veggies, herbs and fruits to eat, why start chomping on daylilies?

However, there's one ornamental plant that does, in my opinion, have culinary merit. That's the nasturtium. The French and Italians think so too. They often mix the peppery-tasting leaves and flowers into salads and also pickle the seeds, which taste like capers. All three have genuine flavor.

So in a city garden with not much room, it's worth planting a few nasturtiums. They are easy to grow and colorful, especially trailing over the sides of containers. They also don't develop big roots that will crowd out your veggies and herbs. And the best part? You're not "wasting space" on these flowers, because almost every part of the nasturtium can be eaten.

Important things to remember

- Nasturtiums need lots of sun to flower well. Water regularly.
- Rich soil is a no-no. Never fertilize. If soil is too rich, they'll produce plenty of leaves but hardly any flowers.
- Some bagged growing mixes and potting soil contain too many nutrients for nasturtiums. Adding a scoop of coarse sand or vermiculite to the mix may help to thin it out.
- There's one drawback to nasturtiums in northern climates. Seeds planted outside after frosts finish don't really get going until halfway through the summer. Provide them with a jump on spring by starting their seeds indoors. But use peat pots, not plastic ones, because nasturtium roots get damaged easily during transplanting. Simply slash the sides of the peat pot and plant the whole thing in the ground or container when the soil warms up.
- If using leaves in salads, pick young green ones. Before using flowers, check carefully for earwigs. They're often lurking inside and taste disgusting.

Nasturtium salad

Wash any kind of salad greens — leaf, Boston, romaine or mesclun mix — then tear leaves into a big salad bowl. Add some ripe, quartered tomatoes and a bunch of washed young nasturtium leaves, stems removed. How many to use depends on personal taste. The leaves taste spicy and can impart quite a zip to salads.

Toss the lot with a vinaigrette made from olive oil, wine vinegar and a teaspoon of Dijon mustard. Ladle onto plates. Top with cubed feta cheese and a few perfect nasturtium flowers.

Oregano *Origanum*

Degree of difficulty
Easy

Needs
Sun. Tolerates some shade

Where
In the ground or a container

When
Perennial. Stays outside
all year

How
Buy started plant.
Seeds take ages

Method
Average soil, preferably
on the sandy side

Problems
Rare. Leaves sometimes
get rust

Harvest
Before the plant flowers

Store
Yes. Dries well

How much to grow
One plant. Oregano
spreads like mad,
so watch it!

Whether you say O-RAY-gunno (as in North America) or O-ri-GARNO (as in Europe), this is one herb that has a strong affinity with Italian cuisine. Its strong, zesty flavor is a standard addition to tomato sauce and pizzas.

And the plant has two big pluses for gardeners. It is easy to grow. Also, it bears the distinction of being one of the very few culinary herbs that tastes better dried than fresh. That means you can harvest bunches of oregano in summertime, then squirrel them away for use all year long.

Oregano's one big drawback is that it spreads. A lot. Your plant will first sprawl unattractively, then cast her seeds at a prodigious rate. I've even seen this bossy herb completely take over a lawn, because the owners weren't vigilant about keeping seedlings under control.

Important things to remember

- Be ruthless with oregano. When you see little ones popping up, get out the trowel and dispatch them pronto.
- In a container, the plant won't be able to spread as much. In fact, you will need to divide the clump every couple of years or so, because if oregano's roots are too confined, leaves turn skimpy.
- Earliest leaves have the best flavor. Cut stalks back hard in early summer, just before they flower. Get out the snippers again later in the season, when new growth has lengthened. Never be afraid to prune oregano!
- Cut stalks go moldy easily. Harvest them on a sunny dry day, after the dew has evaporated.

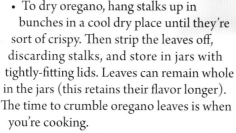

- To dry oregano, hang stalks up in bunches in a cool dry place until they're sort of crispy. Then strip the leaves off, discarding stalks, and store in jars with tightly-fitting lids. Leaves can remain whole in the jars (this retains their flavor longer). The time to crumble oregano leaves is when you're cooking.
- Alternatively, dry oregano in paper bags (large ones — if stalks are too long, cut them in half) with a few holes punched in the sides. Don't cram too many stalks into one bag. They should be loosely packed, allowing the air to circulate.

Recommended varieties

Italian oregano (above right): The original. Strong, unmistakable flavor.

Bristol Cross oregano (opposite): New ornamental variety. Forms a ball-like shape, with striking pink flowers. Looks great in a container. Wimpy flavor, though. For cooking, use the strong Italian kind.

Parsley *Petroselinum crispum*

Degree of difficulty
Can be tricky

Needs
Rich soil, lots of water

Where
In the ground or containers

When
Early spring. Can stay
outside over winter

How
Started plants only.
Seeds take too long

Method
Always trim off yellow
or frizzled-looking stalks.
Water frequently

Problems
Slugs in wet weather

Harvest
When leaves look fully
developed

To store
No. Dried parsley is
tasteless. But chopped
leaves freeze well in ice
cube trays

How much to grow
One plant

Poor parsley. It's usually relegated to a supporting role, as a garnish. Yet this herb's strong, distinctive flavor perks up so many dishes and sauces. The leaves are also loaded with Vitamin C, and chewing parsley after eating garlic helps banish jungle breath. (But watch that a bit of green doesn't get stuck on your teeth. That's a passion killer for sure.)

Gourmet cooks often insist that flat-leafed parsley tastes better than the common crinkly kind. But I personally think this is pure foodie snobbery: there is virtually no difference in flavor between the two.

However, the flat-leafed kind is certainly easier to cook with, because it doesn't keep springing all over the chopping board like its curly, prettier cousin. Italian parsley is also less prone to accumulate annoying gritty soil and dust in among its leaves, because rain washes the detritus off.

Important things to remember

- Parsley is a biennial. That means it produces simply leaves the first year, then flowers the second. After that, the plant dies. If you're growing parsley for culinary use, however, don't worry about this. Just keep snipping leaves off. Then when the plant snuffs it (as it eventually will, usually over winter) go out and buy another started plant.
- This herb is one of the best for containers, but not as easy as many people think. The planting mix must be rich and full of nutrients. It also needs lots of water. Parsley leaves that are turning brown, dried and skimpy mean both requirements are probably lacking.
- The bright green leaves of parsley look very decorative in containers or in a row planted along garden paths.
- If you want parsley to self-seed in the garden, leave the flowerheads on. However, the plant will stop producing edible leaves once this happens.

- Tender new growth tastes best. Keep snipping leaves from the outside to use in cooking. Discard coarse ones.
- Don't bring a parsley plant indoors at summer's end. It's usually worn out and won't produce well. Buy a new started plant.

Recommended varieties

Regular parsley, *P. crispum* (below): Familiar crinky leaves. Looks decorative.

Neapolitan or **Italian parsley**, *P. crispum var. neapolitanum*: Its Plain Jane cousin, with flat leaves. Beloved by foodies.

Peppers, sweet and hot *Capsicum*

Degree of difficulty
Tricky when summer is cool

Needs
Full sun and heat. Water

Where
In the ground or containers at least 18 in. / 45 cm in diameter. One plant per container

When
Spring. Not too early

How
Started plants easiest. From seed, start 10 weeks before final frosts. Keep plants indoors till weather warms

Method
Add scoop of compost to planting holes. Or use nutrient-rich growing mix. Water constantly

Problems
Slugs. Cold weather. Peppers are small and wizened in cool weather

Harvest
When fruits look fully developed

To store
Small hot peppers keep well on strings in a warm dry kitchen. Cut sweet peppers in half, remove seeds, pack flat in plastic bags, store in freezer

How much to grow
One hot pepper plant. Two sweet pepper plants

Peppers are very "in." The huge range of available to gardeners now is astonishing. And while all peppers — both the chile kinds and sweet bell peppers — are semi-tropical, heat-loving plants, if northern summer days and nights are consistently warm, they can produce surprisingly well.

What makes any pepper worth growing is its taste. Virtually all supermarket peppers are now cultivated indoors, hydroponically. Their flavor is okay, for sure. But I find peppers grown outside have a stronger, more satisfying taste — perhaps because they aren't raised in an artificial environment.

Important things to remember

- All peppers like heat, so they're often best grown in containers. If the weather turns cold and rainy, you can haul pots indoors or move them next to a warm wall till the cool spell dissipates.
- In the garden, peppers may wind up puny and bitter-tasting during cold summers. Growing them under row covers or in a greenhouse helps.
- Peppers are very decorative. The plants usually produce a lot of flowers, which should be left as is. Don't be tempted to nip a few flowers off, hoping to encourage "bigger" peppers (as we do with tomatoes). Pepper plants actually perform better if they're

intact. They may send out a second set of flowers later in the season, but these won't usually set fruit in time before the winter.

- In northern summers, small hot peppers are often easier to bring to maturity than the large sweet kind, perhaps because they don't have to swell as big (which requires plenty of sun).
- Plants with small hot ornamental peppers (in all kinds of colors) are now sold everywhere. But for taste, grow real chile peppers.

Recommended varieties

- **Fat 'n Sassy** (left): Big bell pepper. Matures fairly quickly. Progresses from green to red as it ripens.
- **Gypsy**: Elongated sweet pepper. Produces well. Good flavor.
- **Early Jalapeno** (below): Most commonly available hot pepper. Good in cool climates. Progresses from green to red, cute in containers. Spicy enough for most palates.

Potatoes *Solanum tuberosum*

Degree of difficulty
Relatively easy

Needs
Sun. Tolerates some shade

Where
In the ground or deep, wide containers

When
Spring. When soil feels warm to the touch

How
Cut potatoes into pieces, each containing an "eye." Plant about 3 in. / 7.5 cm deep. Needs good soil or nutrient-rich growing mix.

Method
In the ground, make shallow trench mounding up soil around plants as they grow. In containers, start with shallow layer in bottom, then another over cut potato pieces

Problems
Potato beetles, slugs, borers, smelly rot

Harvest
When plants flop over, looking dry and brown

Store
In cool basement. In the fridge, they keep three or four weeks

How much to grow
A few as a treat, if storage facilities aren't available

Why bother with growing spuds when they're so cheap at the supermarket? Three reasons. They taste fantastic. Your own won't have been bombarded with worrying chemicals (so you can safely eat the skins). And it's possible to try unusual varieties that aren't sold commercially.

There's a surprising variety in potatoes now (colors range from golden yellow to a weird purple) and under the right conditions, they do fine. What's great for city gardeners is that they don't mind containers, like a recycled Blue Box. Any wide, roomy one that's about 18 in. / 45 cm deep works. Try using a pile of old car tires too!

Cultivated in this way, potatoes are often easier to dig out than when they're in the ground. And with a loose, nutrient-rich growing mix filling the container, they tend to be better shaped and less prone to disease.

Be careful when digging up spuds that you don't slice into them with a garden fork. It's often better to use a trowel and remove soil a bit at a time.

Important things to remember
- Potatoes rot in cold, wet soil. Wait till all frosts end. Old timers used to pull down their trousers and sit down. If the soil felt warm to bare buttocks, that was the signal to plant.
- Don't cram too many potato pieces in a container. Four is good. Spaced 3 in. / 7.5 cm apart, plants will produce better.

An old recycling box makes a surprisingly good container for growing potatoes, especially small varieties such as French fingerling.

- Farmers till between potato rows, pushing up more soil around plants as they go. Gardeners need to duplicate this process. In the garden: keep scraping soil up around plants or pile straw around the base. In containers: start with a shallow layer of growing mix (lay your potato pieces on top) then layer in more mix. Keep adding more layers as the potato plants grow taller in the container.
- Each potato piece must contain at least one "eye" (a sprout) and preferably two. Before planting, leave cut pieces to dry off for 48 hours, then shake in a paper bag containing a tablespoon of garden sulfur. This helps deter potato beetles and fungal diseases.

Flesh isn't always creamy-colored. Purple-tinted kinds taste good, but go grayish when cooked.

Digging up potatoes is fun — like hunting for buried treasure. Kids love helping, and it's a great way to get them interested in growing things.

- Potatoes from the supermarket are usually sprayed with a growth retardant to stop them sprouting. Seed potatoes from a garden center or specialist supplier give better results.
- Pretty flowers (in violet or white) appear on potato plants after a few weeks. Some then turn into hard green berries, the size of cherry tomatoes. Do not eat these. They are poisonous.
- Dig up potatoes carefully. It is easy to puncture them with a metal trowel. Discard any that feel spongy, have damaged parts or smell funny. The stink of rotting potatoes is one of the worst in the world.

Recommended varieties

- **Purple Viking**: Good all-rounder, purple skin, white flesh. Great boiled or baked.
- **Yukon Gold**: Big, oval shaped, dependable. Absolutely the best for baking in the oven. Stores well.
- **Banana or French fingerling**: Trendy, sausage shaped and small (but you get lots of potatoes), great in containers. A novelty to serve guests.

TASTE TREAT

World's best baked spuds

Oprah Winfrey once said her idea of heaven was "a big baked potato and someone to share it with." Way to go, Oprah. Here's how to achieve at least the first part:

Scrub big Yukon Golds, nicking out any blemishes and spots with a potato peeler. Pat dry with tea towel. Do not wrap in tin foil. Push a metal skewer through each tuber lengthwise (this helps the heat penetrate). Bake in a 400°F / 200°C oven (not the microwave) for an hour or longer, until skin looks sort of crispy and brown.

Remove skewer. Cut open lengthwise, insert a slab of strong cheddar, push sides back together, restore to oven for a minute or two till cheese melts. Serve with thick yogurt or sour cream containing a small chopped handful of dill or parsley, chopped chives and a spoonful of curry powder. And eat the lot. Including, of course, those yummy unsprayed skins, which should be slathered in butter.

Radishes *Raphanus sativus*

Degree of difficulty
Easy

Needs
Sun or partial shade.
Cool conditions

Where
In the ground or a
container

How
Seeds only

When
Early spring

Method
Space seeds of small
varieties 1 in. / 2.5 cm
apart. Allow more space
between bigger kinds

Problems
Wormy invaders
(sometimes)

Harvest
As soon as radishes look
yummy enough to eat

Store
No. They don't keep long

How much to grow
A dozen seeds, interplanted
with something else

Ravishing radishes. Once they were blah and boring, always round and red. But now there's a wonderful array to choose from — elongated two-tone French radishes, fat white Oriental ones, even rainbow varieties that look almost too beautiful to eat.

And radishes are great in a small urban garden, because they grow fast. Some kinds become munchable in less than three weeks. That means you can plant radishes in the same location as seeds of a slower-developing crop such as beans or carrots. Then when the radishes are ready to eat, simply yank them all out and let the beans and carrots take over.

Just for fun, though, allow one radish plant to flower and mature. It will produce curious, long pointed pods which contain edible seeds. In some cultures, these crunchy late bonuses are pickled and used in sauces.

Important things to remember
- Radishes hate heat. Plant early and water if there's no rain.
- Loose soil is important. In clay, radishes don't develop properly. A growing mix in a container often suits them just fine.
- Radishes are a here-today-and-gone-tomorrow kind of veggie. Pick and eat promptly. Old radishes turn tough, fibrous and taste like wads of cotton.

Recommended varieties
French Breakfast: Heirloom variety, trendy, elegant. Oblong, smallish radishes, scarlet with white tips. Mild flavor.
White Icicle: Another hottie. Crisp, mild, quite large. Matures quickly.
Radish Rainbow: Conventional shape and flavor, but extraordinary colors — purple, red, gold, two-tone and white.

Raspberries *Rubus idaeas*

Degree of difficulty
Easy if you have room

Needs
Sun. Some shade okay

Where
In the garden. Not practical in containers

When
Best planted in spring

How
Buy started canes from a garden center

Method
Mix in compost or composted manure first. Dig holes about 3 in. / 8 cm deep, fill with water, stand canes in hole, spreading out roots. Fill and firm the soil so canes stand upright

Problems
Few. Sap beetles on overripe fruit

Harvest
As soon as raspberries look nice and pink. Don't wait

Store
No. Deteriorates quickly. But berries can be frozen

How much to grow
A few canes, as they spread

A h, fresh ripe raspberries. What melt-in-your-mouth flavor and texture! Yet supermarkets don't often stock them and they're pricey. That's not surprising, either, because raspberries are probably the most perishable fruit on the planet. Overnight, even when freshly picked, they can turn squashy, moldy and disgusting.

So grow your own. It's worth doing because the best bet with raspberries is to eat a few perfect ones now and then. Drop these into a bowl of breakfast cereal or a serving of yogurt and the taste is out of this world. And on a summer morning, how wonderful it feels to go outside and pick them.

Everbearing raspberries make this possible. They won't produce a heavy crop all at once, as summer-bearing kinds do. Instead, their growing style is more relaxed. You'll harvest a few berries in June or July, then a trickle more in midsummer, and still more latecomers in the fall. What could be more perfect?

Important things to remember
- Raspberries are best in full sun, although the everbearing kinds cope with some shade.
- They don't like drying out or competition from weeds. A mulch around the base will keep weeds out and moisture in.
- The canes should be trained up something — like a back or side fence with strong, taut wires running up and down. Or provide a free-standing framework.
- Cut out dead canes regularly. Wait till spring, because the dead stuff is more easily recognizable then.
- Raspberries unfortunately sucker everywhere (they travel underground and send up new shoots). Dig these out constantly, removing the roots. And avoid planting anything else too close to a raspberry patch.
- Once raspberries ripen, pick promptly otherwise nasty little picnic bugs will show up. They're black and shiny and feast on fermenting fruit. (They're also called sap beetles or — yikes — *Glischochilis quadrisignatus*.)

A simple but great way to eat raspberries: with thick plain yogurt and perhaps a bit of brown sugar.

Raspberry Custard Pie

This easy recipe comes from my friends Rose Huber and her daughter Ann, who bake it every year using their own berries.

- 1 unbaked pie shell, frozen or make your own
- 2–3 cups raspberries (fresh or frozen)
- 3/4–1 cup (170–225 mL) white sugar
- 2 tbsp. / 25 mL all purpose flour
- 2 eggs
- 1/2 cup / 125 mL cup milk
- 1 tsp. / 5 mL vanilla
- Cinnamon

Pick berries over but don't wash them. Arrange in pie shell. Mix together flour and sugar in bowl. Combine eggs, milk and vanilla in a jug or bowl. Add to the dry mixture. Beat. Pour over berries. Sprinkle cinnamon on top. Bake in preheated 375°F / 190°C oven for 40 minutes, or until custard is firm in center.

Redcurrants *Ribes sativum*

Degree of difficulty
Easy if you have space

Needs
Full sun best. Some shade okay

Where
In the garden. Not suitable for containers unless they're very large and deep

When
Year round. Hardy in northern winters

How
Buy started shrubs in spring

Method
Dig a planting hole 36 in. / 90 cm across. Work composted manure into hole. Fill with water. Let it drain away. Then plant

Problems
Birds. Blister rust

Harvest
When berries turn red

Store
Fresh berries keep only a few days. They freeze well

How much to grow
One shrub, two in a big garden

Few gardeners bother to plant berry bushes nowadays. Yet here's one that's easy to grow, thrives on neglect and churns out clusters of yummy red berries as luscious as shimmering pearls.

Redcurrants are tougher and less prone to disease than their relatives, blackcurrants and whitecurrants. Popular in Scandinavia and Russia, they are perhaps the best fruit to cultivate in a northern backyard.

Use them in a variety of ways and not just for redcurrant jelly, which is tasty but fiddly and doesn't have many uses. Pick and freeze whole berries in empty yogurt containers when the bushes bear fruit, in late June, early July. Then later in the season, combine frozen redcurrants with chopped fresh peaches in a cobbler dessert with a crumble topping. Yum. The strong, sweetish taste of redcurrants is also wonderful in venison stew.

Important things to remember

- A redcurrant bush can grow 4 ft. / 1.2 m high and wide. Allocate a wide space all around it, because you'll need to get at the branches to pick the fruit.
- Prune every year in late winter, before growth starts. Redcurrants bear fruit on branches that are one, two or three years old. Cut older branches out at ground level. Recognizing these "oldies" gets easier the longer you grow redcurrants.
- Birds are a constant nuisance. Drape narrow-gauge plastic netting over bushes when berries start to ripen. Make sure this covering reaches all the way down to the ground. Some feathered visitors are remarkably cunning about finding a way to get underneath.
- Bushes sometimes develop blister rust, which puckers the leaves in ugly red and yellow blotches. But this does not usually affect berry production.

Recommended variety

Red Lake: Developed at the University of Minnesota. Very hardy. Dark red berries.

Ravishing Redcurrant Cake

My own invention — and everyone who tastes the cake does indeed rave about it.

- 3 1/2 cups redcurrants
- 1 tsp. / 5 mL grated orange peel
- 4 tbsp. / 60 mL unsalted butter, softened
- 1/4 cup / 50 mL canola oil
- 1 1/2 cups / 290 g white sugar
- 3 large eggs
- 1 tbsp. / 15 mL baking powder
- 3 1/2 cups / 350 g unbleached white flour
- 1 cup / 250 mL milk

Cream butter and sugar together in a bowl. Mix in oil, add eggs. Beat the mixture till smooth. In a separate bowl, sieve flour and baking powder together. Combine the wet and dry ingredients gradually, adding milk as you go.

Finally fold in redcurrants and orange peel. Pour batter into a 9 in. / 22.5 cm square cake tin with high sides. Bake at 350°F / 180°C for an hour or longer. Test if it's cooked by inserting a dry knife into the center. If wet dough clings to the knife, bake up to another half an hour. (When berries have been harvested wet, cooking takes longer.)

Note: You can also use frozen redcurrants. But don't thaw them before folding into the batter and add at least half an hour to the baking time.

Rhubarb *Rheum x cultorum*

Degree of difficulty
Easy if you have space

Needs
Sun. Some shade okay

Where
In the ground or a container

When
Perennial. Stays outside
all year

How
Buy rhubarb roots in
spring. Don't try from
seed

Method
Allocate an area at least
36 in. / 1 m square in the
garden, preferably more.
Containers must be big
and wide

Problems
Rare

Harvest
In late spring, when stalks
are young and fresh

Store
No. But freezes well

How much to grow
One plant ample

R etro rhubarb is back. Upscale restaurants now feature it on their menus, and that's welcome news. This strongly flavored fruit, a staple of our grandparents, is delicious if it's prepared in the right way.

And it's worth growing your own, because rhubarb is as easy as the proverbial pie made from its pink-tinged stalks. Yet for some reason, those stalks are hard to find, or very pricey, in supermarkets (probably because this is one crop that must be harvested by hand).

Rhubarb also freezes beautifully. Chop what you can't use into 1 in. / 2.5 cm pieces, pack in plastic bags and you'll have a supply on hand all year with no deterioration in flavor.

For very tender rhubarb, some folks put an upturned bucket over the developing plant in early spring. However, timing is crucial because rhubarb shoots up quickly — and I personally think the procedure is overrated.

Important things to remember

- Rhubarb requires room. Leaves get huge. Don't squeeze it into a small space. If using a container, it must be deep and whiskey-barrel wide. Digging the plant out of the container and dividing the roots will be necessary after two or three years.
- Rich soil helps roots develop well. Work composted manure into the area where you're going to plant. Every fall, spread more compost around the base.
- Rhubarb takes a while to get established. You may not see many stalks for a year or two.
- To harvest, grab each stalk low down, twist it slightly, then pull. The stalk should pop neatly out of its "socket."
- If you don't like the taste of rhubarb, grow some anyway, because this is a very handsome plant.

- Leave the plant's towering flower stalks on, to strut their stuff. (Remove these, however, once they start forming, if you want to harvest the fruit.)

TASTE TREAT

Rhubarb cooked in the oven

What puts many people off rhubarb is boiling it on top of the stove. This ruins the texture, turning the firm cut-up chunks into unappetizing stringy mush.

Instead, wash a handful of rhubarb stalks, but don't dry them. Chop these into 1 in. / 2.5 cm pieces and place in a casserole dish without a lid. Add a big scoop of white sugar or more to taste — rhubarb is often very sour — and some grated orange peel. Stir to coat the rhubarb. Cook in the oven on a low heat, about 300°F / 150°C, for an hour.

The rhubarb chunks will stay whole and be bathed in a thickish sauce. Delicious served with plain yogurt or vanilla ice cream.

Rosemary *Rosmarinus officinalis*

Degree of difficulty
Easy in dry summers, sulky in winter

Needs
Mostly sun. Some shade okay

Where
Containers best. Light soil. Adding coarse sand helps

When
Buy plant in spring after frost

How
Started plants only. Seeds take too long

Method
Keep in sun all summer. Move gradually to shade in fall. Bring indoors before frost

Problems
Aphids sometimes. White mold on stems

Harvest
Snip leaves off regularly

Store
Yes. Dries well

How much to grow
One plant is plenty

R avishing rosemary. It's one of the most popular herbs to cultivate in containers — and with good reason. Just ruffle the spiky leaves with your fingers and the powerful resiny aroma wafts everywhere. For me, that unmistakable scent is an instant passport to the Mediterranean shores of Greece and Italy, where rosemary originated. And how wonderful the sensation is during the depths of a gray winter.

The flavor of rosemary is very good with chicken, roast potatoes and on grilled fish. But don't overdo it. This herb packs a punch.

Now grown around the world, rosemary periodically produces pretty bluish violet or pink flowers. It tends to be trouble-free during warm dry summers, but may turn huffy and difficult in rainy, cool weather. And once winter rolls around, watch out!

Important things to remember

- Rosemary is what's called in the gardening trade an "inefficient high light plant." That means it has difficulty adjusting to reduced light conditions indoors during the winter.
- To keep the plant happy, move its pot in early fall to a location that gets half as much sun as where it stood outside in summer. Move the pot again a week later to a spot with even less light. Then give the whole rosemary plant a drastic haircut, followed by a bath in a soap and water solution (see page 28) to banish bugs, and bring it indoors.
- During winter inside, the room should be cool. This is more important than the amount of light. Keep its container quite dry; the plant should stay semi-dormant until spring comes.
- Rosemary sometimes develops a white mold, particularly indoors and during humid weather. This is usually harmless and can be brushed off. Thin out the stems and remove badly affected ones. If the mold gets a serious grip, however, it can kill the plant.

Recommended varieties

- **Common rosemary** *R. officinalis*: The classic kind. Blue flowers. Can grow 3 ft. / 90 cm high, but usually sprawls. Slow to develop in cool climates.
- **Arp rosemary**: The hardiest kind, yet still not hardy enough for northern latitudes. Gray-green foliage.
- **Barbecue rosemary**: A real novelty. Tall straight stems. Can be used as aromatic skewers. May grow 6 ft. / 1.8 m high.

Rosemary kebabs

Cut lengths of barbecue rosemary about 8 in./20 cm long. Snip off most of the spiky leaves, but leave a few here and there and cut a point at one end of each "skewer." Cube chicken breasts, lamb loin or a firm fish.

Cut up chunks of green or red bell pepper and zucchini. Brush everything with olive or canola oil. Push meat on skewers, alternating with the veggie pieces. Grill on medium heat, turning the skewers occasionally for 20 minutes or until done.

Sage *Salvia*

Degree of difficulty
Easy

Needs
Sun. Not too hot. Some shade in afternoons

Where
In the ground or containers

When
Plant early spring, before weather heats up. Perennial, stays outside all year

What
Started plants best. Seeds take too long

How
Provide plenty of space, as sage sprawls. Prune regularly, except in the fall

Problems
Rare for most varieties

Harvest
Snip leaves off as needed, before plant flowers

Store
Yes. Dries well. But fresh leaves can be picked year round

How much to grow
One plant

Sage is a herb that gets mixed reactions. Some people hate the "bitter" taste — but that's probably because the cook used it too liberally in the dish. You can overdo sage very easily when cooking. A little goes a long way.

Yet include sage in your garden, because it's an attractive plant and the cooking kind thrives year round outdoors with no fussing. One big plus for northern gardeners is that the foliage doesn't turn brown and dried-up when winter comes. I have even gone outside on Christmas Eve, brushed snow away, and picked fresh silvery-gray leaves from my sage plant for the turkey stuffing.

Important things to remember
- Sage likes well-drained soil. It will rot in a wet location.
- To keep the plant looking bushy and beautiful, nip out new shoots regularly, otherwise the stems will straggle everywhere and get messy.

- Sage stems become woody with age and need to be cut back. But wield the snippers with caution. Always prune in spring, not fall, and don't go right down to the base of the plant. Whack sage back too hard and you may kill it, particularly in fall.
- This herb is one of the best for drying, because the flavor doesn't diminish. In fact, it gets stronger. Harvested leaves off one plant will probably last you the whole winter.
- To dry sage, cut fresh stems off, put in paper bags with holes poked in the sides, then hang in a warm place. When leaves are sort of crispy, pull them off stems and store in a jar with a lid. Crumble leaves when cooking, not before, as this retains their flavor.

Recommended varieties

Garden sage, *S. officinalis*: Best for cooking and also the hardiest kind. Gray-green leaves, pale blue flowers.

Golden Sage, *S. officinalis* 'Aurea': Yellow leaves, splashed with green. Fetching in a container. Not hardy enough to winter over in most areas.

Tricolor Sage, *S. officinalis* 'Tricolor': White leaves daubed with greenish-gray and pink. Another container-friendly variety. Slightly hardier than 'Aurea'.

Pineapple Sage, *S. elegans*: Trendy tropical herb with red flowers, popular for prettying up cocktails. Crush leaves between your fingers and they really do smell like the tropical fruit. Must be brought indoors for the winter and cut back constantly to stay bushy.

TASTE TREAT

Fried sage leaves

These sound weird, but taste surprisingly good — and are a novelty served with drinks at a party.

- About 20 large fresh sage leaves
- Olive or canola oil
- Salt

Rinse sage leaves. Spread them out individually on a double layer of paper towels. Lay more towels on top and press gently to flatten and dry leaves. Heat about 1/4 in / .6 cm oil in a skillet. When oil starts bubbling, lower heat to medium, then add sage leaves, a few at a time, in a single layer. Fry only until oil stops bubbling around leaves (about 10 to 15 seconds).

Don't let them go brown. Remove carefully with tongs, drain on more paper towels. Sprinkle with salt to taste.

Serve immediately on a dish or store between more paper towels in a container with a lid for no more than 24 hours.

Stevia *Stevia rebaudiana*

Stevia is a much-ballyhooed natural sugar substitute that's gaining more and more fans. Once, only a few health food stores sold the stuff, in powder form, but now you can find powdered or liquid stevia in many drug stores and even supermarkets.

Yet this "magic" sweetener remains pricey, so grow your own. It's quite straightforward, if summers are warm. Originally from subtropical regions of Paraguay and Brazil (where Guarani Indians have used it for years), the plant won't survive northern winters, however. So it's best grown in a container and brought indoors for the winter.

Stevia is truly amazingly sweet. One plant is sufficient. The drawback is that the sweetness (called stevioside) doesn't break down and caramelize in cooking the way sugar does. So dry the leaves, then crumble them finely before use.

Try a pinch of stevia in a cup of coffee first. It has a vaguely cinnamon or licorice flavor. Then get bolder and substitute it in any dish that requires sugar.

Important things to remember

- Stevia hates wet feet. In containers, use a light growing mix and keep the mix moist, but not waterlogged.
- This is a straggly, not-very-pretty plant that's prone to blow over in strong winds. A sheltered, sunny location is best.
- The sweetness is strongest just before the plant produces its little white flowers. Flowering is triggered by shorter days in late summer or early fall. That's the time to harvest.
- Cut the plant almost down to the ground and dry stems and leaves in paper bags, or hang upside down in bunches in a cool but airy basement. When completely dry, strip off leaves, crumble them and store in a clean jar with lid.
- Bring the pot indoors for the winter after a bath in insecticidal soap (see page 28).
- Be warned: A little stevia goes a very long way. To replace one cup of sugar in a recipe, use only a third of a teaspoon of the dried, crumbled leaves.

Recommended variety

Stevia Crazy Sweet, *S. Rebaudiana* 'AC G11A11':
A new strain which has no bitter aftertaste as
regular stevia sometimes does. It is incredibly
sweet, but flavorless.

Developed in Canada, started
plants are available only from
Richters' Herbs. (See
page 121.) For sources of regular
stevia, see page 120.

TASTE TREAT

Fresh stevia tea

This is satisfying
if you're on a diet and craving
something sweet after a meal.
Throw a handful of fresh mint
leaves into a jug or teapot. Add
a couple of stevia leaves, pour
on boiling water, let steep for
5 minutes.

Sip and feel smug that
you aren't consuming any
calories.

Strawberries *Fragaria*

Cultivating local strawberries used to be a hassle, best left to farmers. And pigging out on them was only possible once a year, in early summer.

But that's all changed with "day neutrals" or everybearing strawberry plants. They produce fruit all summer long, right up until fall frosts. These are the best kinds for gardeners to grow.

An everbearing strawberry installed in a container on a sunny deck looks very decorative, except that those delectable little red fruits have a habit of vanishing from the plant. Mine, alas, always get swiped the moment they're ripe — by human visitors or the wild kind (like raccoons).

Important things to remember

- Planting height is critical with strawberries. Too high and the roots will dry out. Too low and they'll rot. And keep roots moist until you're ready to plant.
- Don't let plants dry out over the summer, but don't overwater either. They rot easily. In containers, melting snow pooling on the container surface in early spring will keep the plants waterlogged and probably kill them. So tip the water out.
- Lots of yummy strawberries usually aren't practical in urban spaces because they're space hoggers. But a few are still worth growing for their just-picked sweetness.

- Birds are big pests. Try erecting nets over plants, but it's a hassle and our feathered friends often poke their beaks through the stuff anyway. The best bet is to have a cat. Follow the example of Victorians and put her outside when the berries are ripening. (They used to tether squads of kitties in among rows of strawberries to keep birds away.) But nowadays, watch out for horrified neighbors.

Fresh strawberries with yogurt and brown sugar

I think simple is best with these berries, especially if you only have a precious few to savor. I can't be bothered to fiddle around with strawberry shortcake, because I'm always too impatient to eat them.

Wash berries but don't nip the green tops off. Put a pool of thick plain full-cream yogurt (not low fat) on a big plate, next to a little pile of demerara brown sugar. Eat strawberries with your fingers, dipping them in the sugar first, then yogurt. Summer treats don't get any better than this.

Summer Savory *Satureja hortensis*

Degree of difficulty
Easy

Needs
Sun. Light, sandy soil

Where
In the ground or containers

When
Outside after frost.
Annual herb. Won't survive
northern winters

How
Seeds. Started plants
often hard to find

Method
Don't start indoors.
Just cover seeds with a
smidgen of soil in the
garden. Or use containers
at least 6 in. / 15 cm wide.
One plant per container

Problems
Rare

Harvest
Keep snipping leaves off.
Don't let it flower

Store
Yes. Dries well, but tastes
better fresh

How much to grow
One plant

Known as the "bean herb" because its distinctive flavor is perfect with fresh green beans, summer savory is one of the oldest known culinary seasonings. Originally from the shores of the Mediterranean, it was popular with earlier generations, yet few gardeners seem familiar with its virtues today.

That's too bad because summer savory is easy to grow, looks decorative in a container and perks up any kind of bean dish. Try it with lentils, kidney and white beans, even chick peas. It's also good with soups, sauerkraut, meat, fish and eggs.

Important things to remember

- Summer savory doesn't like being transplanted. Sow it directly into the garden or a container.
- It grows quickly into a low, bushy plant. Keep cutting the twiggy stems off if you want to use the leaves in cooking. Don't let flowers form (even though they are pale blue, delicate and pretty).
- Bees like summer savory. Growing it is a good way to attract several kinds of pollinating insects to your garden.
- The leaves are tiny, but don't leave them whole. They must be chopped or crushed to release the aromatic oils in cooking.
- At summer's end, it isn't worth bringing a container of summer savory indoors. Leaves will soon become too skimpy to use. Far better to dry the herb for winter use.

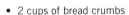

TASTE TREAT

Summer savory chicken stuffing
Recipe contributed by Bona Vista Summer Savory farm
in Belle River, Prince Edward Island, Canada

- 2 cups of bread crumbs
- 2 tsp. / 10 mL dried or fresh summer savory (or to taste)
- 2 tbsp. / 25 mL melted butter
- 1 medium onion chopped
- 1 tsp. / 5 mL salt

Combine ingredients and insert stuffing into chicken cavity.
Roast as usual.

Thyme *Thymus*

Degree of difficulty
Can be cranky

Needs
Sun. Dry location

Where
In the ground or container

When
Perennial. Stays outside
all year

How
Buy started plant. Seeds
take ages

Method
Doesn't mind poor soil.
Likes sand

Problems
Rare

Harvest
Before the plant flowers

Store
Yes. Dries well

How much to grow
Two or three plants

Make time for thyme. More gardeners should grow this aromatic herb. Not as trendy as basil and oregano, it is second to none in any cuisine which uses chicken or fish.

And along with standard cooking thyme (favored by the French) you can find many novelty varieties, including caraway thyme, lavender thyme and rose petal thyme.

Most are easy to grow, with two qualifiers. First, the plant must receive sun most of the day. Second, the location should be dry.

And bear in mind that leaves of all thymes are tiny. You don't get an awful lot on each plant. Strip these off the twiggy stems at the end of summer and you'll wind up with barely a handful. So if you want to cook with thyme throughout the winter, it's a good idea to have several plants.

Important things to remember

- Thyme hates shade and anywhere soil is moist or boggy.
- The best location is often a rock garden in full sun, or alongside a dry concrete pathway. Squeeze the roots in between stones or cracks in paths. Thyme usually settles in and is perfectly happy.
- If using a container, don't fill it with a nutrient-rich mix, or one that is formulated to retain water. Adding a scoop of coarse builder's sand will help create the right dry environment. Some people grow thyme successfully in pure gravel.
- The plant needs very little moisture. Don't overwater.
- If you want to use thyme in cooking, nip flower buds off.
- In areas with little or no snow cover, put a mulch around the base of the plant, but remove it promptly in spring or roots will rot.

Recommended varieties

Common thyme, *T. vulgaris*: Still the best for cooking.

Lemon thyme, *T. x citriodorus*: Several kinds. Lovely fragrance. The golden version, '*Aureus*', is decorative in containers.

Lemon Carpet, *T. herba-barona* does well between paving stones. Can spread everywhere and become a nuisance.

Woolly thyme, *T. pseudolanuginosus*: Dense, low-growing carpets of grayish green leaves, furry as an angora sweater. Slow to develop. Fun to stroke.

Broadleaf Thyme, *Plectranthus amboinicus* (below): Tropical, decorative. Big soft, strokable leaves. Not really a thyme at all, but has a similar flavor. Popular in Jamaican and Latin American cooking. Looks pretty in a container. Must be brought indoors for the winter.

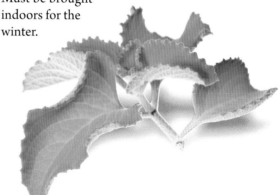

Tomatillos *Physalis ixocarpa*

What fun tomatillos are — easy to grow, fascinating to look at. And if you're into Mexican food, they're sensational in salsas.

These are not, as many people think, little tomatoes, but an entirely different plant. The edible part — the tomatillo — comes wrapped in its own papery "lantern," which gradually expands like a balloon being blown up. You must peel off this husk before boiling or roasting the round, shiny, green fruits that are stashed away like treasure inside.

And tomatillos have one huge plus: they are usually blissfully free of bugs, because slugs, earwigs and other creepy crawlies can't easily penetrate those protective husks.

Important things to remember

- Plant two, to ensure germination.
- Tomatillo plants spread wide. Leave 4 ft. / 120 cm between each plant and let them sprawl. If using containers, they should be whiskey-barrel size or wider. The soil doesn't have to be deep.
- Pick fruits before their protective husks start to go brown and papery looking. Left too long on the plant, the fruit will split.
- Most tomatillo varieties produce green fruit, which swell to cherry tomato size or larger and turn a paler green when completely ripe. There is also a purple variety.

Salsa verde

Imparts a true taste of Mexico, unlike many bland bottled salsas made with tomatoes. And it's fat free.

- About a dozen tomatillos, husked and rinsed
- 1 small chopped onion
- 3 mashed cloves of garlic
- 1 or 2 hot peppers, seeds removed, roughly chopped
- Handful of fresh cilantro or Vietnamese coriander leaves (see page 117)

Peel husks off tomatillos and discard. Rinse tomatillos under running cold water to remove the sticky coating, which is always present. Place in saucepan, cover with cold water (some tomatillos will float) and simmer for about 10 minutes until fruits are olive green and about to burst. Drain, leave to cool.

Combine in blender the onion, garlic, hot peppers, cilantro and salt to taste. Whirl. Add tomatillos and whirl again till smooth. Serve in dipping dishes, with tortilla chips. ¡Delicioso!

Tomatoes for Containers
Lycopersicon esculentum

Degree of difficulty
Easy

Needs
Sun all day

Where
Wide, deep containers, at least 18 in. / 45 cm in diameter. Plastic grow bags also work

When
Spring, after frost

How
Started plants easiest. From seed, sow indoors six weeks before last frost

Method
Provide supports within the container (obelisks, bamboo stakes, tree branches) or a trellis on a wall or fence behind

Special requirements
Regular watering. Nutrient-rich growing mix

Problems
Few

Harvest
From 60 to 100 days, depending on the variety

Store
Use up quickly. They don't keep well

How much to grow
Two or three plants

On patios, decks and balconies, think small. Cherry or patio kinds of tomatoes are by far the best to grow. Regular tomatoes — the ones with fruit that's golfball-sized or bigger — may produce lots of foliage in containers, but harvests can be skimpy.

This is especially true of heirloom varieties, which seem to hate being confined to pots. Heirlooms are also prone to disease. See pages 114–115.

However, small doesn't have to mean ho-hum. Forget those tiresome Tiny Tim tomatoes of yesteryear. There are dozens of cherry varieties to choose from now, plus a few "patio" kinds which are a little bigger.

Important things to remember

- All tomatoes require plenty of water and sun. Don't let containers dry out.
- They are very sensitive to cold. If late frosts are threatened, throw a light cotton sheet (not plastic) over containers at night, making sure every stem and leaf is covered. Remove the sheet promptly in the morning. Do the same thing if the temperature drops near zero in early fall, when fruits are ripening.
- As tomato plants develop, conventional wisdom is to nip out the "suckers" which appear in the fork between the main stem and new "branches." But if you forget or are too lazy, like me, don't fret. You'll wind up with a bushier plant, but still get some fruit.

- Tie plants to supports with something soft, like torn-up rag strips or old pantyhose. Don't use string or wire.
- Good ventilation is important, but tomatoes don't like wind. On a balcony or deck provide a sheltered spot.
- Don't overload with fertilizer, but do use a growing mix rich in organic matter. One formulated especially for tomatoes is good.

Recommended varieties

- **Container Superbush**: Not a cherry or patio variety, but large fruits on sturdy stems. Developed especially for containers. Delicious.
- **Juliet**: Grape-shaped, quite large, sweet. Very prolific.
- **Sweet Million**: Another prolific variety. Huge numbers of small, sweet, pop-in-the-mouth fruits, which are prone to crack when ripe.
- **Whippersnapper** (above): Very early heirloom tomato, matures in 60 days or less. Surprisingly hassle free. Loads of small, round, rosy red fruit.

Heirloom Tomatoes
Lycopersicon esculentum

Degree of difficulty
Can be tricky

Needs
Sun all day, steady
temperatures

Where
Preferably in the ground

When
Spring, after frost

How
Started plants easiest.
From seed they take ages

Method
Put supports in the ground
first, then dig holes. Add
scoop of compost to holes
before planting. Fish
emulsion (mixed into the
watering can) helps in the
initial stages, but don't
overfertilize

Special requirements
Regular and even watering.
Don't splash water on
leaves. Keep roots moist
with a mulch around base

Problems
Unfortunately, yes

Harvest
From 80 to 110 days
after planting

Store
In a cool, dry place,
not the fridge

How much to grow
Depends. Some heirlooms
produce a few huge fruit.
Others are smaller and
more prolific

Plain red tomatoes? Boring, boring... Heirloom kinds are all the rage now. They're colorful — deep purple to pineapple yellow to rainbow stripes — and often oddly shaped. Their names are fascinating too: Radiator Charlie's Mortgage Lifter, Sicilian Saucer, Lunchbucket, Pink Accordion ....

And the ballyhoo about their superior flavor does seem justified. It's sometimes sweet, sometimes sharp, always very "tomato-ey." Flesh may burst with juice or be quite dry, like a Roma paste tomato.

However, heirlooms can be cantankerous. If this is your first attempt at tomatoes, hedge your bets and plant a modern hybrid variety as well.

Black Krim variety

Tomato woes

Slugs attack all tomatoes in wet weather. Huge, scary-looking critters called hornworms may also make a surprise appearance on foliage. Both are easy to control. Just pick off and squash.

With heirlooms, however, the big bugaboo is fungal diseases. Most varieties are susceptible in fluctuating weather conditions (such as hot sunshine followed by cool rainy periods). Late blight *Phytophthora infestans* is the worst offender. Once it hits, there's no cure. You have to pull up plants and burn or put them in the garbage. Don't compost.

Signs of disease: Discolored leaves and stunted growth. In late summer, dark blotches on foliage, leaves curling up, and brownish areas on fruit, which quickly become soft and smelly or hard and calloused. To ward blight off, snip off excess foliage earlier in the season. Don't let developing tomatoes get smothered in among wet leaves. And if there's even a hint of blight on the leaves, pick all the fruit, then soak the lot in the sink in a solution of bleach and water. That may save a few.

Popular Brandywine is particularly prone to disease. Skip it in areas which experience high humidity.

Another nasty affliction: fruits with squashy and blackish bottoms. These have succumbed to blossom end rot, which can usually be blamed on changeable weather. And there is no cure.

Important things to remember

- Heirlooms need lots of room, often becoming massive plants. Snip tops off if they're still skybound late in the season.
- Many heirlooms take an eternity to mature. That means, in the north, you may be lucky to harvest before fall frosts arrive.
- Because they're oddly shaped and often large, heirlooms don't keep as long as other tomatoes. Use up quickly or dry them.
- Cracking on top is common and these damaged bits, which look awful, must be cut off before eating. But the flesh still tastes fine underneath.

Recommended varieties

- **Black Krim**: Brownish flesh with lots of seeds. Odd reddish-brown skin often stays green on top. From the Ukraine. Grows well, fantastic flavor, prolific.
- **Costoluto** (preceding page): Means "ribbed" in Italian. Ridgy sides, weird shapes, delicious. The first tomatoes to be introduced to Europe from North America in the 16th century. Good for drying.
- **Persimmon**: Pineapple color, dates from the 1800s. Mid- to big-sized fruits, produces well. Yummy once you get used the idea of eating yellow tomatoes.

TASTE TREAT

Your own sundried tomatoes

Firm varieties like Costoluto are best. (Don't use any which have very juicy flesh when you cut them open.) Halve tomatoes lengthwise, scrape out seeds. Place on baking sheet, skin side down, sprinkle with salt, bake in oven at 200°F / 100°C for up to 12 hours. Peek occasionally! When ready, they should have the texture of a raisin and feel dry, but not crisp. You may need to turn the slices over once or twice.

Cool, pack tightly in plastic bags, removing all air. Store in freezer for up to a year. To rehydrate: soak tomatoes, barely covered, in hot water mixed with olive oil for 5 to 10 minutes. Use like canned tomatoes. The liquid left behind can be added to soups.

Vietnamese Coriander
Polygonum odoratum

Degree of difficulty
Easy

Needs
Sun

Where
In a container.
This is a tropical plant

When
Anytime

From seed
No

How
Container, should
preferably be at least
1 ft. / 30 cm wide

Method
Bring indoors for the
winter. Plant may need
dividing after a year
or two

Problems
Rare

Harvest
Snip off fresh leaves
for cooking.

Store
No. Doesn't
dry well

**How much to
grow**
One plant is
ample

Regular coriander or cilantro (the kind sold in bunches at supermarkets) is a royal pain to grow. The plants shoot up too fast and their frilly, edible leaves keep getting smaller. In order to have a fresh supply on hand, you must keep sowing fresh seed every few weeks.

Who wants the hassle? Try this alternative instead. Grown in a pot, Vietnamese coriander is trouble free and tastes remarkably similar to the regular kind.

Known by many names — Chinese parsley, Cambodian mint and laksa leaf — the plant hails from Indochina and is related to a common weed that grows everywhere. It's no raving beauty in the garden. However, the arrow-shaped leaves and reddish stems have an exotic smell and flavor that's both lemony and spicy. They make a perfect accompaniment to many cuisines, including Oriental, Indian and Mexican.

Important things to remember
- Don't let this plant flower if you want to cook with it. Keep cutting so it stays bushy. Stems turn long and straggly quickly.
- In cooking, use the leaves only. Stalks are tough.
- Keep the pot moist. Leave outside in summer. Come winter, administer a haircut and bath (see page 28) and bring indoors to the sunniest spot you can find.

Zucchini / Courgette *Cucurbita pepo*

Degree of difficulty
A cinch if you have space

Needs
Sun all day. Heat

Where
In the ground or a big container

When
Outside after soil has warmed up

How
Seeds only

Method
Make a mound in the soil. Plant four seeds. Thin to one. In a container, thin to only one too

Problems
Rare

Harvest
Before they turn into torpedoes

Store
No. Doesn't keep long

How much to grow
One plant

This veggie (also called courgette) is the butt of many jokes. It's tasteless. It swells as big as baseball bats. People flee when they see a zucchini-toting gardener coming. And so on.

Yet grow it anyway, because it's fun: ridiculously easy, striking to look at, and so fast, you'll be fascinated. On early summer mornings, I can't wait to go out and check how my jet-propelled zucchini plant is coming along.

However, all squashes are problematic in the city because they need a truckload of space. Don't bother with zucchini if you can't provide an area at least 36 in. / 90 cm square or a deep container that's whiskey-barrel size or larger. And even if you can, go for a container-friendly or climbing variety.

Important things to remember

- Zucchini likes heat. In northern climates, spread out a large piece of black plastic over the growing area. (Buy this by the yard at a hardware store.) Punch a hole 12 in. / 30 cm square in the plastic, mound up a scoop of compost within the hole, plant seeds there. The plastic helps retain heat and keeps weeds down.
- Seeds rot in cold, wet soil. Always wait till nights are above 65°F / 18°C before planting.
- Don't cram plants close together. One per hole is best.
- Try to cut zucchini off the plant when they're no more than 4 in. / 10 cm long. The older, the tougher, and the skin turns bitter. Cutting also encourages the plant to set more fruit.
- In wet summers, pollination may be skimpy because bees are scarce. So do the job yourself. With a small

paintbrush, remove pollen from male flowers (which have one lone pistil sticking up) and brush it on to the female flowers (whose centers are divided into four segments).

- Humid weather late in the season may trigger unsightly white mold on zucchini leaves. But this doesn't usually affect the fruit.

Recommended varieties

- **Portofino** (also called Largo, Striato or Romanesco) (left): Popular in Italy. Ridged sides. Absolutely the most flavorful zucchini you can grow.
- **Black Forest F1 Hybrid**: Touted as the first climbing zucchini. Needs a strong fence or trellis for support, as the central stem grows thick and heavy.
- **Summer Ball F1 Hybrid**: A novelty. Round yellow fruit like mini-pumpkins. One of the few zucchini suitable for containers.

TASTE TREAT

Sweet and sour zucchini

This recipe comes from Kathy Hewett, vegetarian cook and avid gardener who lives Stoke Edith, Herefordshire, England. She likes to use Clarita, a Lebanese-type zucchini with pale green skin, grown in her own garden, but says any zucchini works well.

- 3 or 4 medium zucchini, sliced
- 3-4 tbsp. / 45–60 mL olive oil
- 1/2 tsp. / 15 mL cinnamon
- 2 tbsp. / 25 mL white wine vinegar
- 1 tbsp. / 15 mL sugar
- 2 tsp. / 10 mL pine nuts
- Pepper

Sprinkle zucchini with salt and leave to drain in a colander for an hour. Pat dry. Sauté in oil in frying pan, then cover and cook till tender. Season with pepper and cinnamon. Pour in vinegar, sugar and pine nuts. Raise heat slightly, flip slices gently and cook until sauce turns syrupy. Serves 4.

Seed and Plant Sources

Started plants

Use these whenever possible, because they will mature quicker than seeds. But be sure to buy them from a reputable garden center. You need strong, healthy plants that have been given a good start in life — not weak, spindly ones that may be diseased or infested with bugs.

Some seed suppliers listed below sell started plants by mail order — and if the plant is unusual (or grown from cuttings, not seeds), they're worth buying. But bear in mind that many veggie and herb seedlings are perishable and won't benefit from sitting around in a cardboard box at the post office.

Seeds

Seed catalogues have varying strengths. One may offer a great range of runner beans and tomatoes, but be hopeless for herbs. Another may be the opposite. Some have well designed indexes so a certain item is easy to find. Others make you rummage through page after page to locate what you're looking for.

Whatever their individual delights and drawbacks, all catalogues are fun, because we usually thumb through them during the winter. And there's nothing nicer than fantasizing about next spring's garden on a chilly day! Whether you intend ordering on line, by phone or by snail mail, look at lots of catalogues. The print ones are usually free (one of the best bargains around, in fact) and very entertaining.

I recommend the following suppliers, for differing reasons. Use the code at the end of each address to locate a specific item featured in this book. However, remember that their offerings can change from year to year.

William Dam Seeds
279 Highway 8, RR 1
Dundas, Ontario
L9H 5E1
Canada
Color catalogue
All organic, untreated seeds
(Canada) 1-905-628-6641
www.damseeds.com
Will ship seeds to U.K.
DAM

Dominion Seed House
P.O. Box 2500
Georgetown, Ontario
L7G 5L6
Canada
Color catalogue, good instructions
1-800-282-5746
www.dominion-seed-house.com
DOM

Gardenimport
P.O. Box 760
Richmond Hill, Ontario
L4B 4R7
Canada
Canadian supplier of some Sutton seeds
Beautiful catalogue
1-800-339-8314
www.gardenimport.com
GAR

Jekka's Herb Farm
Rose Cottage, Shellard Lane
Alveston, Bristol
BS35 3SY
U.K.
Herbs only. All organic. Extensive selection
01454-418878 or 0845-2903255
www.jekkasherbfarm.com
JEK

Johnny's Selected Seeds
955 Benton Ave.
Winslow, Maine
04901-2601
Great catalogue. Clear instructions
(U.S.) 877-JOHNNYS (564-6697)
(Canada) 1-877-JOHNNYS (564-6697)
Johnnyseeds.com
Will ship seeds to U.K.
JOHN

Marshalls Seeds
Alconbury Hill
Huntingdon, Cambridgeshire
PE28 4HY
U.K.
Great website
Award-winning color catalogue
01480-443390
www.marshalls-seeds.co.uk
MAR

Nicky's Nursery
Fairfield Road
Broadstairs, Kent
CT10 2JU
U.K.
Heirloom veggies and herbs
01843-600972
www.nickys-nursery.co.uk
NICK

Peppers by Post
West Bexington
Dorchester, Dorset
DT2 9DD
U.K.
Hot peppers galore
01308 897766
peppersbypost.biz
Will ship seeds to U.S. and Canada
PEP

Renee's Garden Seeds
6060 Graham Hill Road, Suite A
Felton, California
95018
U.S.A
Beautiful seed packets. Interesting
varieties
(U.S.) 888-880-7228
(Canada) 1-888-880-7228
On-line sales only
Does not ship to Europe
reneesgarden.com
REN

Richters
Goodwood, Ontario
L0C 1A0
Canada
Huge variety of worldwide herbs
Comprehensive catalogue
1-800-668-4372
www.richters.com
Ships seeds to Europe
RIC

Rogueland's, U.K.
On-line sales only
Great selection of heirloom tomatoes
www.seedfest.uk
ROG

Sea Spring Seeds
West Bexington
Dorchester, Dorset
DT2 9DD
U.K.
Unusual herbs and veggies
01308-897766
www.seaspringseeds.co.uk
Will ship seeds to U.S. and Canada
SEA

Stokes Seeds
P.O. Box 10
Thorold, Ontario
L2V 5E9
Canada
Large company, new varieties every year
(U.S.) 800-396-9238
(Canada) 1-800-396-9238
www.stokeseeds.com
STO

Sutton Seeds
Woodview Road
Paignton, Devon
TQ4 7NG
U.K.
Large company, interesting varieties
0844-9220606
www.suttons.co.uk
SUT

T & T Seeds
Box 1710
Winnipeg, Manitoba
R3C 3P6
Canada
Limited selection, good cold climate
varieties
Color catalogue
204-895-0964
www.ttseeds.com
T&T

Terra Edibles
Box 164
Foxboro, Ontario
K0K 2B0
Canada
Small, family owned
B&W catalogue
Heirloom varieties only
On-line sales only
613-961-0654
www.terraedibles.ca
TERRA

Territorial Seeds
P.O. Box 158
Cottage Grove, Oregon
OR 97424
Terrific growing instructions
Print catalogues only in the U.S.
(U.S.) 800-626-0866
(Canada) 1-800-626-0866
www.territorialseed.com
TERRI

Thompson & Morgan
Large company, dependable new
varieties
Comprehensive color catalogue
U.K.
Poplar Lane
Ipswich, Suffolk
1P8 3BU
0844-2485383
www.thompson-morgan.com
U.S.
800-274-7333
www.tmseeds.com
Canada
47-220 Wyecroft Road
P.O. Box 306
Oakville, Ontario L6J 5A2
1-877-545-4386
www.thompsonmorgan.ca
T&M

Veseys Seeds
P.O. Box 9000
Charlottetown, Prince Edward Island
C1A 8K6
Canada
Color catalogue, clear instructions
1-800-363-7333
www.veseys.com
VES

If you're looking for...

Asparagus peas, page 34. DAM, GAR, SUT, T&M, TERRI, VES

Basil, page 36.
Sweet, Genovese, Bush, Green Globe: DAM, JEK, JOHN, MAR, RIC, STO. Also at many garden centers.
Thai, Spice, Siam Queen: JEK, JOHN, RIC, STO, TERRI.
Magical Michael: REN, RIC, STO
Purple Ruffles: JEK, JOHN, MAR, REN, RIC, JOHN, STO. VES. Also at many garden centers.
Mrs. Burns Lemon: JEK, JOHN, RIC VES
Lesbos: RIC (Started plants only. Cannot be grown from seed.)

Runner or pole beans, page 38.
Runner Bean Wisley Magic, page 39. T&M exclusive
Royal Burgundy: DAM, JOHN, STO, T&M, TERRI

Beets, page 40.
Pablo: MAR, VES
Red Ace: Most seed companies
Chioggia: DAM, JOHN, MAR, REN, STO, T&M TERRI, VES

Carrots, page 42.
Nantes: Most seed companies
Resistafly: MAR, T&M
Chantenay: Most seed companies
Mignon: MAR, REN, STO, T&M, TERRI (Thumbelina and Parmex are similar).
Rainbow: DAM, JOHN, MAR, REN, VES
Purple Haze: DAM, DOM, MAR, REN, STO, T&T, TERRI

Catnip, page 44.
Regular catnip: DOM, JEK, JOHN, RIC, VES
Lemon catnip: JEK, RIC

Celeriac, page 46. Most seed companies.

Chard (also called Swiss chard), page 50.
Bright Lights: sold everywhere
Pot of Gold: REN exclusive

Cucumbers, page 52.
Fanfare: DAM, MAR, STO, SUT, T&M, VES
Container Bush Slicer: REN
Lemon: JOHN, MAR, SUT, T&T, T&M, TERRA, TERRI
Armenian: JOHN, TERRI

Dill, page 54. Sold everywhere.

Edamame (also called Soybeans), page 56. T&M, TERRA, TERRI

Eggplant (also called aubergine) page 58.
Little Prince: REN (Alternative: Calliope, T&M; or Ophelia, MAR, SUT)
Fairy Tale: DAM, DOM,TERRI, VES

Epazote, page 60. JOHN, RIC, SEA, TERRI

Fava beans (also called broad beans), page 62. JOHN, MARSH, SUT, T&M, VES

Ground cherries (also called cape gooseberries) page 66. DAM, JOHN, T&M, TERRI, VES

Lettuce, page 68.
Tom Thumb: MAR, REN, SUT, T&M
Leaf Lettuce mixtures: all seed companies
Freckles: REN, T&M

Lime/Lemon balm, page 70. JEK, RIC, SEA

Melons, page 72.
Alaska muskmelon:T&T, VES
Earlisweet muskmelon: DAM, DOM, JOHN, STO, T&M

Mesclun Mix, page 74. Most seed companies.

Mojito mint, page 78. RIC. (Alternative: JEK Lime mint)

Nasturtiums, page 80. All seed companies.

Oregano, page 82.
Italian or Greek: sold everywhere
Bristol Cross: RIC

Peppers, page 86.
Fat 'n Sassy: PEP, T&T, VES (Alternative: Ace, MAR)
Gypsy: DAM, PEP, T&M, VES
Jalapeno: Most seed companies

Potatoes, page 88. Most companies sell seed potatoes. Kinds available can vary from year to year.

Radishes, page 91.
French Breakfast: DAM, JOHN, MAR, REN, RIC, SUT, T&M, T&T, TERRI, VES
White Icicle: JOHN, TERRI VES
Radish Rainbow: JOHN, T&M

Rosemary, page 98.
Common rosemary: sold everywhere
Arp rosemary: JEK, RIC, SEA, TERRI
Barbecue rosemary: RIC, TERRI

Sage, page 100: Buying a started plant at a garden center is best.
For seeds:
Garden sage: most garden centers
Golden sage: JEK, RIC
Tricolor sage: JEK, NIC, RIC
Pineapple sage: JEK, NIC, RIC

Stevia, page 102.
Regular stevia: DAM, JEK, RIC. SEA, TERRI
Supersweet stevia: RIC

Summer savory, page 106. Most seed companies.

Thyme, page 108.
Regular thyme: sold everywhere
Lemon Thyme, JEK, RIC, SEA
Lemon Carpet Thyme: JEK, RIC, SEA
Woolly Thyme: JEK, RIC
Broadleaf Thyme: RIC, SEA

Tomatillos, page 110. DAM, JOHN, RIC, SEA, T&M, TERRI, VES

Tomatoes for containers, page 112.
Container Superbush: REN
Juliet: DAM, JOHN, STO, T&M, T&T, VES
Sweet Million: TERRI, VES
Whippersnapper. TERRA (Alternative: Tumbling Tom. T&M, VES)

Tomatoes, heirloom, page 114.
Black Krim (also called Black Russian or Black Prince) DAM, JOHN, NICK, REN, ROG, SEA, T&M, TERRA, TERRI
Costoluto: REN, ROG, T&M,
Persimmon: REN, TERRA, TERRI

Vietnamese coriander, page 117. RIC. (Alternative: cilantro, sold by most seed suppliers.)

Zucchini (also called courgette), page 118.
Portofino: DAM, DOM, JOHN, REN, T&M, TERRI, VES
Black Forest Fl Climbing Hybrid: T&M
Summer Ball F1 Hybrid: REN, DOM (Alternative: Eight ball DOM, JOHN, STO, TERRI)

Index

Photo credits

All photographs by Barrie Murdock unless otherwise noted.

Thanks to the additional suppliers whose photographs have been featured in this book, including Renee's Garden (page 12 bottom, 21) and Richter's Herbs (page 83 right).

The following photographs copyright © iStockphoto and the individual photographers (page numbers follow names): Leviticus (2-3); Kkgas (8, 18); Claus Mikosch (9); Joan Kimball (10); Liza McCorkle (11 top and bottom, 37, 51); Joe Klune (12); Henry Hazboun (13); Laura Stone (14 left); Lisa Santore (14 right); Barbara Helgason (15); Chris Price (16, 88, 97 top); Danie Nel (17 top); Tyler Stalman (19); Kelly Cline (20); Tina Rencelj (22 top); Jill Chen (22 middle); Maurice van der Velden (23, 32, 112); René Mansi (24 top right); Nicolas Loran (24 bottom left); Rick Wylie (26 top); T.W. van Urk (26 middle); C J McKendry (26 bottom); Michael Pettigrew (27 left); Martin Firus (27 top middle); alohaspirit (27 bottom right); Vincent Voight (29); Rod Pforr (30 left); Greg Banks (31); Alina Solovyova-Vincent (33); William Berry (55); Tanya F (57 bottom); Sololos (58); FotografiaBasica (71); CostinT (75); Elena Talberg (79); Anne Clark (81); Antonia D'Albore (83 bottom left); Fred Didier (85 top); Ivonne Wierink-vanWetten (93 top); Неля Смирнова (94); Chris Elwell (97 bottom); Togoshi (99 top); Valeria Titovia (100); Daniel Norman (109); Patricia Gower (116); Dirk Richter (119 top); Hedda Gjerpen (120).